ANALYZING THE ISSUES

CRITICAL PERSPECTIVES ON THE COLLEGE ADMISSIONS PROCESS

Edited by Bridey Heing and Greg Baldino

Enslow Publishing

101 W. 23rd Street
Suite 240
New York, NY 10011
USA

enslow.com

Published in 2018 by Enslow Publishing, LLC
101 W. 23rd Street, Suite 240, New York, NY 10011

Library of Congress Cataloging-in-Publication Data

Names: Heing, Bridey, editor. | Baldino, Greg, editor.
Title: Critical perspectives on the college admissions process / edited by Bridey Heing, Greg Baldino.
Description: New York : Enslow Publishing, 2018. | Series: Analyzing the issues | Includes bibliographical references and index. | Audience: Grades 9-12.
Identifiers: LCCN 2017005455 | ISBN 9780766084797 (library bound)
Subjects: LCSH: Universities and colleges--United States--Admission--Juvenile literature. | College choice--United States--Juvenile literature.
Classification: LCC LB2351.2 C76 2018 | DDC 378.73--dc23
LC record available at https://lccn.loc.gov/2017005455

Printed in China

To Our Readers: We have done our best to make sure all website addresses in this book were active and appropriate when we went to press. However, the author and the publisher have no control over and assume no liability for the material available on those websites or on any websites they may link to. Any comments or suggestions can be sent by email to customerservice@enslow.com.

Excerpts and articles have been reproduced with the permission of the copyright holders.

Photo Credits: Cover, Rawpixel.com/Shutterstock.com (college students), Thaiview/Shutterstock.com (background, pp. 4–5 background), gbreezy/Shutterstock.com (magnifying glass on spine); p. 4 Ghornstern/Shutterstock.com (header design element, chapter start background throughout book).

CONTENTS

INTRODUCTION

The first few months of autumn are a time of excitement and anxiety for many high school seniors as they face the question, "Where will I go to college?" It's an energetic time for colleges, too, as their admissions counselors meet with prospective students at college fairs and in one-on-one meetings to find the next generation of college freshmen for their institution. College admissions is a complex process, taking into account not only the students as they are now, but who they could become. Every school is looking for their future alumni and every prospective student is looking for his or her future alma mater.

The first and most obvious factor in admissions is a student's record of academic performance. Grades and standardized test scores are thought of as one of the most important indicators of being a good student, but there are other things to be taken into account. What a college or university expects out of its students is different from a high school, and good grades do not automatically translate into college readiness. College courses can take the form of independently directed laboratory classes or lecture classes where a student may be one of hundreds who never directly interact with the instructor. Classes like this require a different skill set than smaller, more hands-on learning environments. Different departments will also have varying standards for what they're looking for: an interdisciplinary humanities program is going to be looking for something different than a science, technology, engineering, and math (STEM) program.

Cost is also an important factor in the decision process. College can be expensive to the point of inaccessibility. Community colleges are often the most reasonable, but are usually limited in what kind of degrees they can provide. Different types of financial aid are available, but with different limits and requirements. Student loans can cover most or all of college expenses, even including dormitory housing and food, but have to be repaid with high interest rates. A good academic record can open eligibility for grants and scholarships, but there is also funding available for people based on their background. These funding programs can range from the G. I. Bill, for military veterans, to support for people from low-income families. If an applicant isn't eligible for financial aid, they may be turned down because the school feels they wouldn't be able to keep up with tuition costs.

There's a third factor that applies to college admissions, as well, which is not something that can be found on paper: What is the character of the prospective student, and how will they fit into the culture of the institution to which they are applying? At a public college or big university this may not be as much of a factor, but for smaller and private schools this can be just as important as a grade point average (GPA). These are things that can be revealed in an application essay, or an interview with an admissions counselor.

Getting into college can be a complicated and difficult process, but it is also the first step on an important journey. For many career fields, there's simply no way to get hired without a degree. Even some service jobs require applicants to have at least a four-year degree. Graduating college is also something that many people find personally fulfilling, and most people agree that access to education is important for all citizens. But the best way to open those doors is a topic of heated debate, with a great deal of controversy surrounding topics ranging from how admissions decisions should be made to how to allocate funding for students. This book will explore the many solutions, opinions, and debates surrounding college admissions to provide a comprehensive look at how we as a society are ensuring everyone has access to higher education.

CHAPTER 1

WHAT THE EXPERTS SAY

When the admissions cycle starts, it's not just students who are eager to apply to universities and colleges. Those institutions are also eagerly seeking out potential applicants. Every fall counselors reach out to prospective students, hoping to find the right match for their school and to draw a diverse pool of candidates. But since it is impossible for schools to know who will perform best, they have to rely on past performance to predict the future—a tricky business that many fear are leaving strong candidates behind. The articles in this chapter examine the ways in which colleges work at adjusting their standards to ensure all students receive an equal opportunity, as well as refocusing their selection process to find the students who will be best suited for their programs.

EXCERPT FROM "BARS TO EDUCATION: THE USE OF CRIMINAL HISTORY INFORMATION IN COLLEGE ADMISSIONS," BY REBECCA R. RAMASWAMY, FROM THE *COLUMBIA JOURNAL OF RACE AND LAW*, 2015

I. INTRODUCTION

It was such a chilling effect. To think that I wanted to go to college and here, as I'm on my path to change my life, I'm still being asked these questions.

—Glenn Martin
Founder and President,
JustLeadershipUSA (Incarcerated 6 years)[1]

In this era of mass incarceration and tough-on-crime policies in the United States, it is becoming increasingly common for Americans to have some form of involvement with the criminal justice system. Records of this involvement can have serious implications for individuals even after they have completed their punishments. Legal scholars have extensively explored employers' use of such records in hiring decisions, and a small number of claims have been brought against this practice, with limited success.[2] An issue that has received less scholarly and legal attention is the prevalence of the use of criminal justice involvement screenings to inform admissions decisions for colleges and universities.[3]

When the Center for Community Alternatives conducted a survey of colleges and universities, a majority of the 273 respondents—sixty-six percent—reported that they collect criminal justice information from their applicants in admissions proceedings.[4] Twenty-five percent of the responding schools reported that they impose an automatic bar to admission in at least some criminal-justice-related circumstances,[5] and forty percent stated that they would not admit an applicant who is currently completing a term of community supervision.[6] About thirty-three percent reported that pending misdemeanors or misdemeanor arrests can hurt an application, and eleven percent stated that they viewed "lesser-offense youthful offender adjudications" in a negative light.[7] Based on this survey, the Center for Community Alternatives concluded that

> screening of college applicants is becoming increasingly common; that people with criminal records are subjected to special admissions screening procedures; that college personnel other than admissions officials often participate in the admissions decision; that a wide range of criminal convictions and even arrests can negatively impact the admissions decision; that failure to disclose a conviction can result in rejection or expulsion; and that even after admission, students with records may be subject to special restrictions.[8]

Civil rights laws do not provide any special protection for people with criminal records, but the well documented racial disparities within the criminal justice system create a close relationship between intentional discrimination against people with criminal justice involvement and unintentional discrimination on the basis of race.[9] The potential legal vulnerability of this admissions practice is a race-based disparate impact claim under Title VI of the Civil Rights Act (which prohibits discrimination on the basis of race, color, or ethnicity by organizations receiving federal funding) brought by the Department of Education's (DOE) Office for Civil Rights.

This Note argues that colleges and universities that receive federal funding may be vulnerable to a race based disparate impact claim under Title VI of the Civil Rights Act if they use records of applicants' criminal histories to inform admissions decisions. Part I draws the connection between intentional discrimination on the basis of criminal histories and unintentional discrimination on the basis of race. It explores the implications of the entrenched racial disparities within the criminal justice system as well as some of the myriad consequences of criminal justice system involvement and the role of education in overcoming their harmful effects. Part II begins with an overview of how the Equal Employment Opportunity Commission (EEOC) has used disparate impact claims under Title VII to challenge employment discrimination against people with criminal histories. The second half of Part II explores the DOE's ability to bring disparate impact claims through its Title VI authority in the context of higher education. Part III develops the disparate impact legal claim that could be brought if the DOE used the strategy that the EEOC has used in employment cases under Title VII to attack this discrimination in higher education under Title VI.

1. Do you think it is fair that criminal justice screenings are used in college admissions?

2. What groups of students, in particular, might this affect the most? Why?

"THE MISSING 'ONE-OFFS': THE HIDDEN SUPPLY OF HIGH-ACHIEVING, LOW-INCOME STUDENTS," BY CYNTHIA THALER, FROM *JOURNALIST'S RESOURCE*, APRIL 17, 2013

Many of the most selective colleges in the United States have policies that now make tuition free or very inexpensive for low-income students. This includes Harvard, Yale, Princeton and Stanford. Low-income students who achieve high academic standards are highly desirable applicants for these institutions. But it turns out that most of these students — who typically benefit the most from **selective schools** — do not end up applying to colleges that would be a proper "match" with their academic talents.

A December 2012 study for the Brookings Institution and the National Bureau of Economic Research, "The Missing 'One-Offs': The Hidden Supply of High Achieving, Low Income Students," quantifies this disjunction between selective colleges and the low-income high achievers they might enroll. The authors, based at Stanford University and the Harvard Kennedy School, make a distinction between low-income, high-achieving students who apply to selective institutions ("achievement-typical") and those who do not ("income-typical" behavior). They define "high achieving" students as those who score in the top 10% on their college aptitude test (SAT or ACT). "Low-income" is defined as any high school senior whose estimated family income is at or below $41,472, or the bottom 25% of the 2008 family income distribution. "High income" is defined as a student whose family income is above $120,776, or in the top 25% of the 2008 family income distribution. The scholars draw on data from the Census Bureau, the College Board and the National Student Clearinghouse, among other organizations.

The study's findings include:

- Most high-achieving, low-income students do not apply to any selective universities. These are students whose demonstrated college-testing aptitude is almost identical to that of high-achieving students from wealthy families. About two-thirds of this low-income, high-achieving group does not end up attending one of the nation's more than 200 selective colleges.
- Only 8% of "low-income, high-achieving students apply in a manner that is somewhat close to what is recommended and to what their high-income counterparts do: they apply to at least one match college, at least one safety college with median scores not more than 15 percentiles lower than their own, and apply to no non-selective colleges."
- Thirty-nine percent of "low-income, high-achieving student use application strategies that an expert would probably regard as odd. It is not unusual, for instance, to see students who apply to only a local

non-selective college and one extremely selective and well-known college — Harvard, for instance."

- "Income-typical students do not come from families or neighborhoods that are more disadvantaged than those of achievement-typical students. However, in contrast to the achievement-typical students, the income-typical students come from districts too small to support selective public high schools, are not in a critical mass of fellow high achievers, and are unlikely to encounter a teacher or schoolmate from an older cohort who attended a selective college."
- The study's authors also assert that this "phenomenon occurs because many colleges are 'searching under the lamp-post.' That is, many colleges look for low-income students where the college is instead of looking for low-income students where the students are."
- Seventy percent of the achievement-typical students "come from just fifteen urban areas: San Francisco, Oakland, Los Angeles, San Diego, Dallas, Houston, Chicago, Cleveland, Pittsburgh, Portland, Boston, Providence, New York, Philadelphia, and Baltimore. Only 21% of achievement-typical students live in a non-urban area (not necessarily rural, but a town rather than an urban area suburb)."
- Among the group of low-income higher achievers, 15.4% are "underrepresented minorities," and 15.2% are Asian.
- The data show that a "student's being an under-represented minority is not a good proxy for his being low-income. Thus, if a college wants its student body to exhibit income diversity commensurate with the income diversity among high achievers, it cannot possibly attain

this goal simply by recruiting students who are underrepresented minorities. If admissions staff do most of their outreach to low-income students by visiting schools that are largely Hispanic and black, the staff should realize that this strategy is likely to lead to a student body that is not income-diverse."

The authors conclude that the students in question are "insufficiently geographically concentrated to be reached, cost-effectively, by popular methods of informing students about their college opportunities: visits by admissions staff to high schools, campus visits by students, after school college access programs, contact with teachers who attended selective colleges, and the like."

1. What does the research show about high-achieving, low-income students? What makes them different from higher-income students?

2. How can admissions teams at selective schools encourage these high-achieving students to apply?

"THE ADMISSION ARMS RACE: SIX WAYS COLLEGES GAME THEIR NUMBERS," BY MARIAN WANG, FROM *PROPUBLICA*, APRIL 23, 2013

As college-bound students weigh their options, they often look to the various statistics that universities trumpet — things like the high number of applications, high test scores, and low acceptance rate.

But students may want to consider yet another piece of info: the ways in which schools can pump up their stats.

"There's no question about it," said David Kalsbeek, senior vice president for enrollment management and marketing at DePaul University. "There are ways of inflating a metric to improve perceived measures of quality."

Some of these tweaks — such as a more stream-lined application — can actually benefit students. Others serve to make the admissions process more confusing. Here's a rundown.

1) QUICKIE, OFTEN PRE-FILLED OUT APPLICATIONS

Express applications — sometimes known as "fast apps," "snap apps," "V.I.P. applications" or "priority applications" — are often pre-filled with some student information and require little if anything in the way of essays. And especially when they're accompanied with an application-fee waiver, what's a student got to lose? Not much, fans of fast apps argue.

The school, meanwhile, has a lot to gain. The tactic, designed to broaden the pool of applicants, can help super-charge application numbers. Drexel University and St. John's University — the only two private colleges among the top 10 for most applied-to colleges in 2011 — both market broadly and use fast apps.

Both schools received roughly 50,000 applications in the fall of 2011, according to U.S. News data. Both schools enroll roughly 3,000 freshmen.

Getting in more applications can also boost the appearance of selectivity. Critics contend that some schools use fast apps specifically for this purpose — luring students into apply to institutions they hadn't heard of and ultimately rejecting a portion of them. Neither school, when contacted, responded to requests for comment.

2) SHORTER APPLICATIONS, COMMON APPLICATIONS, AND SHORTER COMMON APPLICATIONS

Another way to get more applications is to adopt the Common Application, as nearly 500 colleges have since its inception in 1975. The form, which lets students apply to multiple schools at once, has fueled the long-term rise in applications. And as more colleges have adopted it, other schools have felt pressure to start using it too.

Many schools have long required that students submitting a Common Application include additional answers or essays. Dropping the extra requirements can result in a spike in applications. That's what happened for Skidmore College, which saw a 42 percent jump in applications this cycle after it stopped requiring supplemental essays to the Common App. (Skidmore College's dean of admissions did not respond to a request for an interview.)

3) DIPPING INTO EARLY APPLICATION POOLS

Another statistic schools often try to control is their "yield" — that's admissions parlance for the percentage of students offered admission that choose to attend.

Though it's no longer statistically factored into U.S. News & World Report's ubiquitous rankings, yield rates are still a data point made available to prospective students. They're also inextricably tied to acceptance rates because schools use previous yields to calculate how many students they should admit to fill a class. Schools with low yields must extend lots of acceptances, knowing many accepted students will go elsewhere.

One way to increase yields is to draw heavily from the pool of applicants who chose to apply through early action, or to encourage early decision, which is binding. At the University of Pennsylvania, for instance, nearly half of the spots in the freshman class are filled through the university's binding early decision process.

Penn is hardly alone in leaning heavily on early decision. Many schools accept early decision applicants at a higher rate than students who apply later. American University, for instance, accepts about 75 percent of early decision applicants, though its overall acceptance rate is far lower.

One other thing to note: Because early decision involves committing before any financial aid is offered, it generally attracts wealthier families. Students who need financial aid or want to be able to make cost comparisons between different schools are typically advised not to apply early — which can hurt their chances.

4) REJECTING GOOD STUDENTS UNIVERSITIES THINK ARE JUST USING THEM AS A BACKUP

While opening up early decision and early action programs is a way for colleges to force students to demonstrate that they're their top choice, schools use a variety of ways to

17

divine the same information from regular decision students as well. This is perhaps the most common — and in some ways, common sense — method used by colleges to improve yield: simply to admit only those students who they perceive as likely to enroll.

"There are so many silent electronic footprints they're leaving nowadays," said Sundar Kumarasamy, vice president for enrollment management and marketing at the University of Dayton.

Kumarasamy said that his institution tracks many of these subtle signals of interest from applicants: They can tell whether individual applicants clicked to open email communications, logged into the system to check the status of an application, and not only whether they called the school, but how long that phone call lasted. If the school gets the sense that an applicant isn't interested, that's factored in. Kumarasamy calls it "recruiting for fit."

The interest — or lack thereof — can ultimately mean that the school rejects some candidates who on paper are more than qualified but failed to demonstrate interest.

5) MAKING TESTS OPTIONAL

One admissions trend within the past decade has been the test-optional movement. Colleges that have stopped requiring standardized test scores often cite equity and diversity as reasons to make the move, noting the strong correlation between socioeconomic status and test scores.

But going test-optional can also help universities' stats. Critics note that in addition to attracting more applicants, the move ultimately skews the average test scores that institutions report: Lower-scoring applicants are the most likely to withhold their scores and higher-scoring applicants are the most likely to submit them.

6) MAKING STUFF UP

Some colleges actually cross the line with their creative number-crunching. Since the start of last year, five colleges have acknowledged overstating their admissions statistics: Bucknell University, Claremont McKenna College, Emory University, George Washington University, and Tulane University's business school.

Admissions data is self-reported and no outside party is responsible for verifying it. The recent scandals involving falsified data have only come to light after colleges disclosed the problems themselves.

U.S. News' Robert Morse has said there is "no reason to believe that the misreporting is widespread." But a survey by Inside Higher Ed last fall suggests that even admissions directors are skeptical of the reporting, with 91 percent of those surveyed saying believe they believe there's more misreporting than has been identified.

Of course, some colleges resist the pressure to pump up admissions numbers. Doing so is unusual enough that it attracts notice and media write-ups.

Boston College made "a strategic decision" this cycle to raise the admissions bar by adding an essay. It got the expected drop in applications — and a recent write-up in the *New York Times*. A handful of others, including Ursinus College, have done the same. In addition to requiring essays again, they dropped the fast app.

But for many other colleges, what's been called the admissions "arms race" is on — with these strategically achieved statistics as the scoreboard.

1. Should colleges ask whether they are a backup choice on admissions forms? How might this benefit students for whom the school in question is their first choice?

2. What are the benefits of a more involved application process compared with the advantages of in-depth personal interviews? How could shortcuts in either area benefit the other?

"AFFIRMATIVE ACTION IN UNIVERSITY ADMISSIONS: RESEARCH ROUNDUP," BY ALEXANDRA RAPHEL, FROM *JOURNALIST'S RESOURCE*, DECEMBER 9, 2015

In April 2014, the U.S. Supreme Court upheld a Michigan constitutional amendment banning affirmative action policies in the state's universities. The ruling follows up on *Fisher v. University of Texas*, a 2013 case in which the Court declined to make a comprehensive judgment on affirmative action, sending the case back to a lower court with instructions to apply "strict scrutiny" to the use of race in admissions.

The plaintiff in the 2013 case was Abigail Fisher, a white student who was denied admission to the University of Texas at Austin in 2008. Texas residents ranked at the top of their high school class (usually the top 10%) are eligible for automatic admission and fill 75% of the available in-state spots. Those who do not meet this qualification are admitted based on factors such as academic achievement, extracurricular activities, cultural background and race. Fisher, who was part of the second group, believed that she was denied admission because of her race, claiming that several of her non-white high school classmates were admitted despite having lower grades. Her legal team argued that this is a violation of the 14th Amendment's equal protection clause and Title VI of the Civil Rights Act of 1964.

The United States District Court heard *Fisher v. University of Texas* in 2009 and ruled in favor of the university, as did the United States Court of Appeals for the Fifth Circuit in 2011. In February 2012 the Supreme Court agreed to hear the case and oral arguments took place in October 2012. The ruling in the case would technically only apply to public universities; but if the Court had ruled that affirmative action programs constitute racial discrimination, private universities would likely also be forbidden from using race in admission under Title VI of the Civil Rights Act of 1964, which forbids racial discrimination in all programs that receive federal funding. (For more on this case, you can read the official transcript of the oral arguments as well as consult the SCOTUSblog.)

The case is only the latest wrinkle in a decades-old legal battle: In the 1978 case *University of California Regents v. Bakke*, the U.S. Supreme Court ruled that some affirmative action admissions programs were constitutional, but that race-based quotas were not. In a famous pair of cases in 2003 — *Grutter v. Bollinger* and *Gratz v. Bollinger* — the Court affirmed the right of the University of Michigan Law School to consider race as part of a "holistic review" of an application. At the same time, the Court ruled that the school's undergraduate process, which automatically awarded 20 points to minority applicants, was unconstitutional. In two 2007 cases, *Parents Involved in Community Schools v. Seattle School District No. 1* and *Meredith v. Jefferson County Board of Education*, the Court ruled against programs that sought to use race as a "tiebreaker" for admission to oversubscribed public schools.

Research has shown that diversity experiences at college can have positive effects for students' civic growth and their healthy participation in a globalized world. But even if institutions of higher education only used family income, not race, as their chief criterion for diversity, many structural challenges would remain. High school students from low-income families of all races are less likely to apply to universities. A 2012 study from Stanford University and the Harvard Kennedy School found that the "vast majority of very high-achieving students who are low-income do not apply to any selective college or university."

Below are several of the latest studies that examine some of the issues of affirmative action in university admissions and bias:

"AFFIRMATIVE ACTION AND THE QUALITY-FIT TRADEOFF"

Arcidiacono, Peter; Lovenheim, Michael. National Bureau of Economic Research working paper, February 2015.

Summary: "This paper reviews the literature on affirmative action in undergraduate education and law schools, focusing in particular on the tradeoff between the quality of an institution and the fit between a school and a student. We first discuss the conditions under which affirmative action for under-represented minorities (URM) could help or harm their educational outcomes. We then provide descriptive evidence on the extent of affirmative action in law schools, as well as a review of the contentious literature on how affirmative action affects URM student performance in law school. We present a simple selection model that we argue provides a useful framework for interpreting the disparate findings in this literature. The paper then turns to a similar discussion of affirmative action in undergraduate admissions, focusing on evidence of the extent of race-based admissions practices and the effect such preferences have on the quality of schools in which minority students enroll, graduation rates, college major and earnings. We pay much attention to the evidence from state-level bans on affirmative action and argue these bans are very informative about how affirmative action affects URM students. Finally, we discuss the evidence on "percent plans," which several states have enacted in an attempt to replace affirmative action."

"AFFIRMATIVE ACTION AND ITS MYTHOLOGY"

Fryer Jr., Roland G.; Loury, Glenn C. National Bureau of Economic Research working paper, July 2005.

Summary: "For more than three decades, critics and supporters of affirmative action have fought for the moral high ground — through ballot initiatives and lawsuits, in state legislatures, and in varied courts of public opinion. The goal of thispaperistoshowtheclarifyingpowerofeconomicreasoning to dispel some myths and misconceptions in the racial affirmative action debates. We enumerate seven commonly held (but mistaken) views one often encounters in the folklore about affirmative action (affirmative action may involve goals and timelines, but not quotas, e.g.). Simple economic arguments reveal these seven views to be more myth than fact."

"IS THERE A 'WORKABLE' RACE-NEUTRAL ALTERNATIVE TO AFFIRMATIVE ACTION IN COLLEGE ADMISSIONS?"

Long, Mark C. *Journal of Policy Analysis and Management*, 2014. doi: 10.1002/pam.21800.

Abstract: "The 2013 decision by the U.S. Supreme Court in the *Fisher v. University of Texas at Austin* case clarified when and how it is legally permissible for universities to use an applicant's race or ethnicity in its admissions decisions. The court concluded that such use is permissible when 'no workable race-neutral alternatives would produce the educational benefits of diversity.' This paper shows that replacing traditional affirmative action with a system that uses an applicant's predicted likelihood of being an underrepresented racial minority as a proxy for the applicant's actual minority status can yield an admitted class that has a lower predicted grade point average and likelihood of graduating than the class that would have been admitted using traditional affirmative action. This result suggests that race-neutral alternatives may not be 'workable' from the university's perspective."

"ASSESSING THE POTENTIAL IMPACT OF A NATIONWIDE CLASS-BASED AFFIRMATIVE ACTION SYSTEM"

Xiang, Alice; Rubin, Donald B. *Statistical Science*, 2015, Vol. 30. doi: 10.1214/15-STS514.

Abstract: "We examine the possible consequences of a change in law school admissions in the United States from an affirmative action system based on race to one based on socioeconomic class. Using data from the 1991–1996 Law School Admission Council Bar Passage Study, students were reassigned attendance by simulation to law school tiers by transferring the affirmative action advantage for black students to students from low socioeconomic backgrounds. The hypothetical academic outcomes for the students were then multiply-imputed to quantify the uncertainty of the resulting estimates. The analysis predicts dramatic decreases in the numbers of black students in top law school tiers, suggesting that class-based affirmative action is insufficient to maintain racial diversity in prestigious law schools. Furthermore, there appear to be no statistically significant changes in the graduation and bar passage rates of students in any demographic group. The results thus provide evidence that, other than increasing their representation in upper tiers, current affirmative action policies relative to a socioeconomic-based system neither substantially help nor harm minority academic outcomes, contradicting the predictions of the "mismatch" hypothesis, which asserts otherwise."

"AFFIRMATIVE ACTION BANS AND THE 'CHILLING EFFECT'"

Antonovics, Kate L.; Sander, Richard H. *American Law and Economics Review*, 2013, doi: 10.1093/aler/ahs020.

Abstract: "This paper examines whether California's Proposition 209, which led to the 1998 ban on the use of racial preferences in admissions at the University of California (UC) system, lowered the value that underrepresented minorities placed on attending UC schools. In particular, we look for evidence of a chilling effect in minority yield rates (the probability of enrolling in a UC school conditional on being accepted) after Proposition 209. Using individual-level data on every freshman applicant to the UC system from 1995 to 2000, we find no evidence that yield rates fell for minorities relative to other students after Proposition 209, even after controlling for changes in student characteristics and changes in the set of UC schools to which students were admitted. In fact, our analysis suggests Proposition 209 had a modest 'warming effect.' We investigate and rule out the possibility that this warming effect was driven by changes in the selection of students who applied to the UC, changes in financial aid or changes in minorities' college opportunities outside the UC system. Instead, we present evidence consistent with the idea that Proposition 209 increased the signaling value of attending UC schools for minorities."

"THE EFFECTS OF AFFIRMATIVE ACTION BANS ON COLLEGE ENROLLMENT, EDUCATIONAL ATTAINMENT AND THE DEMOGRAPHIC COMPOSITION OF UNIVERSITIES"

Hinrichs, Peter. *Review of Economics and Statistics*, August 2012, Vol. 94, No. 3. doi:10.1162/REST_a_00170.

Abstract: "I estimate the effects of affirmative action bans on college enrollment, educational attainment, and college demographic composition by exploiting time and state variation in bans. I find that bans have no effect on the typical student and the typical college, but they decrease underrepresented minority enrollment and increase white enrollment at selective colleges. In addition, I use the case study methods of Abadie and Gardeazabal (2003) and Abadie, Diamond, and Hainmueller (2010) and find that the affirmative action ban in California shifted underrepresented minority students from more selective campuses to less selective ones at the University of California."

"A COMPARATIVE ANALYSIS OF AFFIRMATIVE ACTION IN THE UNITED KINGDOM AND UNITED STATES"

Archibong, Uduak; Sharps, Phyllis W. *Journal of Psychological Issues in Organizational Cultures*, July 2011, Vol. 2, No. 2., 17-38. doi: 10.1002/jpoc.

Abstract: "Based on research conducted during a large-scale European Commission project on international perspectives on positive/affirmative action measures, the authors provide a comparative analysis of the legal context and perceptions of the impact of positive action in the United Kingdom and the United States. The study adopted participatory methods including consensus workshops, interviews, and legal analysis to obtain data from those individuals responsible for designing and implementing positive action measures. Findings are discussed, conclusions drawn, and wide-ranging recommendations are made at governmental and organizational levels. The authors conclude by suggesting possible implications for policy and argue for widespread awareness-raising campaigns of both the need for positive action measures for disadvantaged groups and the benefits of such measures for wider society. They also recommend the adoption of a more coherent and collaborative approach to the utilization and evaluation of the effectiveness of positive or affirmative action."

"WHEN WHITE PEOPLE REPORT RACIAL DISCRIMINATION: THE ROLE OF REGION, RELIGION AND POLITICS"

Mayrl, Damon; Saperstein, Aliya. *Social Science Research*, December 2012. doi: 10.1016/j.ssresearch.2012.12.007.

Abstract: "Scholarly interest in the correlates and consequences of perceived discrimination has grown exponentially in recent years, yet, despite increased legal and media attention to claims of 'anti-white bias,' empirical studies predicting reports of racial discrimination by white

Americans remain limited. Using data from the 2006 Portraits of American Life Study, we find that evangelical Protestantism increases the odds that whites will report experiencing racial discrimination, even after controlling for racial context and an array of social and psychological characteristics. However, this effect is limited to the South. Outside the South, political affiliation trumps religion, yielding distinct regional profiles of discrimination reporters. These findings suggest that institutions may function as regional "carriers" for whites inclined to report racial discrimination.

"RACE AND AFFIRMING OPPORTUNITY IN THE BARACK OBAMA ERA"

Wilson, William Julius. *Du Bois Review*, 2012, 9:1, 5-16. doi: 10.10170S1742058X12000240.

Abstract: "I first discuss the Obama administration's efforts to promote racial diversity on college campuses in the face of recent court challenges to affirmative action. I then analyze opposition in this country to 'racial preferences' as a way to overcome inequality. I follow that with a discussion of why class-based affirmative action, as a response to cries from conservatives to abolish 'racial preferences,' would not be an adequate substitute for race-based affirmative action. Instead of class-based affirmative action, I present an argument for opportunity enhancing affirmative action programs that rely on flexible, merit-based criteria of evaluation as opposed to numerical guidelines or quotas. Using the term 'affirmative opportunity' to describe such programs, I illustrate their application with three cases: the University of California, Irvine's revised affirmative action admissions procedure; the

University of Michigan Law School's affirmative action program, which was upheld by the Supreme Court in 2003; and the hiring and promotion of faculty of color at colleges and universities as seen in how I myself benefited from a type of affirmative action based on flexible merit-based criteria at the University of Chicago in the early 1970s. I conclude by relating affirmative opportunity programs for people of color to the important principle of 'equality of life chances.'"

"AFFIRMATIVE MERITOCRACY"

Walton, Gregory M.; Spencer, Steven J.; Erman, Sam. *Social Issues and Policy Review.*

Abstract: "We argue that in important circumstances meritocracy can be realized only through a specific form of affirmative action we call affirmative meritocracy. These circumstances arise because common measures of academic performance systematically underestimate the intellectual ability and potential of members of negatively stereotyped groups (e.g., non-Asian ethnic minorities, women in quantitative fields). This bias results not from the content of performance measures but from common contexts in which performance measures are assessed — from psychological threats like stereotype threat that are pervasive in academic settings, and which undermine the performance of people from negatively stereotyped groups. To overcome this bias, school and work settings should be changed to reduce stereotype threat. In such environments, admitting or hiring more members of devalued groups would promote meritocracy, diversity, and organizational performance. Evidence for this bias, its causes, magnitude, remedies, and implications for social policy and for law are discussed."

"THE MARLEY HYPOTHESIS: DENIAL OF RACISM REFLECTS IGNORANCE OF HISTORY"

Adams, Glenn; Nelson, Jessica C.; Salter, Phia S. *Psychological Science*, December 2012. doi: 10.1177/0956797612451466.

Abstract: "This study used a signal detection paradigm to explore the *Marley hypothesis* — that group differences in perception of racism reflect dominant-group denial of and ignorance about the extent of past racism. White American students from a midwestern university and black American students from two historically black universities completed surveys about their historical knowledge and perception of racism. Relative to black participants, White participants perceived less racism in both isolated incidents and systemic manifestations of racism. They also performed worse on a measure of historical knowledge (i.e., they did not discriminate historical fact from fiction), and this group difference in historical knowledge mediated the differences in perception of racism. Racial identity relevance moderated group differences in perception of systemic manifestations of racism (but not isolated incidents), such that group differences were stronger among participants who scored higher on a measure of racial identity relevance. The results help illuminate the importance of *epistemologies of ignorance*: cultural-psychological tools that afford denial of and inaction about injustice."

"RACIAL MISMATCH IN THE CLASSROOM: BEYOND BLACK-WHITE DIFFERENCES"

McGrady, Patrick B.; Reynolds, John R. *Sociology of Education*, January 2013, Vol. 86, No. 1, 3-17. doi: 10.1177/0038040712444857.

Abstract: "Previous research demonstrates that students taught by teachers of the same race and ethnicity receive more positive behavioral evaluations than students taught by teachers of a different race/ethnicity. Many researchers view these findings as evidence that teachers, mainly white teachers, are racially biased due to preferences stemming from racial stereotypes that depict some groups as more academically oriented than others. Most of this research has been based on comparisons of only black and white students and teachers and does not directly test if other nonwhite students fare better when taught by nonwhite teachers. Analyses of Asian, black, Hispanic and white 10th graders in the 2002 Education Longitudinal Study confirm that the effects of mismatch often depend on the racial/ethnic statuses of both the teacher and the student, controlling for a variety of school and student characteristics. Among students with white teachers, Asian students are usually viewed more positively than white students, while black students are perceived more negatively. White teachers' perceptions of Hispanic students do not typically differ from those of white students. Post-estimation comparisons of slopes indicate that Asian students benefit (perceptionwise) from having white teachers, but they reveal surprisingly few instances when black students would benefit (again, perceptionwise) from having more nonwhite teachers."

"BELIEFS ABOUT AFFIRMATIVE ACTION: A TEST OF THE GROUP SELF-INTEREST AND RACISM BELIEFS MODELS"

Oh, Euna; Choi, Chun-Chung; Neville, Helen A.; Anderson, Carolyn J.; Landrum-Brown, Joycelyn.

Journal of Diversity in Higher Education, 2010, Vol. 3, No. 3, 163-176. doi: 10.1037/a0019799.

Abstract: "Two models of affirmative action attitudes (i.e., group self-interest and racism beliefs) were examined among a sample of racially diverse college students. Open-ended questions were included to provide students an opportunity to elaborate on their beliefs about affirmative action and beliefs about the existence of racial discrimination. Findings from logistic regression analysis on a subsample ($n = 376$) provide support for both models; race (a proxy for group self-interest) and racism beliefs (as measured by the Color-Blind Racial Attitudes Scale [CoBRAS] and an open-ended question) helped predict endorsement of affirmative action in theoretically expected ways. Asian, Latino and black students were more likely to view affirmative action as helpful compared to their white counterparts, and limited awareness of institutional racism (i.e., higher CoBRAS scores) was associated with antiaffirmative action arguments. Follow-up analysis, however, provided support for the superiority of the racism beliefs model as measured by the CoBRAS in predicting affirmative action beliefs over the group-interest model. Limitations and implications for future research are discussed."

"WHAT LIES BENEATH SEEMINGLY POSITIVE CAMPUS CLIMATE RESULTS: INSTITUTIONAL SEXISM, RACISM AND MALE HOSTILITY TOWARD EQUITY INITIATIVES AND LIBERAL BIAS"

Vaccaro, Annemarie. *Equity & Excellence in Education*, 2010, Vol. 43, No. 2, 202-215. doi: 10.1080/10665680903520231.

Introduction: "In an effort to make higher education institutions more welcoming spaces, many campuses engage in climate assessment. Campus climate study results can provide valuable insight into the state of a university and offer direction for climate improvements. This article offers a feminist analysis of climate data that emerged from the open-ended comment section on a campus climate survey. By using a critical feminist lens, the researcher uncovered 'what lies beneath' seemingly positive quantitative results. Qualitative results revealed male hostility toward diversity initiatives, resentment toward liberal bias, symbolic racism, and institutional sexism."

1. What do these studies tell us about affirmative action? How do the findings compare and contrast?

"TIPPING POINT FOR TRANS ADMISSIONS? SMITH COLLEGE WILL NOW ACCEPT TRANSGENDER APPLICANTS WHO IDENTIFY AS WOMEN. WILL OTHER WOMEN'S COLLEGES FOLLOW?" BY SCOTT JASCHIK, FROM *INSIDE HIGHER ED*, MAY 4, 2015

Smith College's board on Saturday approved an admissions policy that explicitly welcomes applications from transgender people who identify as female.

The move by Smith, which follows similar shifts by several other leading women's colleges, is seen by some as a likely turning point in the fight by transgender women and their many allies at women's colleges to make those institutions welcoming of all who identify as women. For a long time, many women's colleges have had some students who are admitted and enroll as women, but who come to identify as men and transition toward that identity. And most women's colleges (Smith among them) have supported and retained such students. For those who were not born women, women's colleges have historically refused admission.

A joint statement from Kathleen McCartney, Smith's president, and Elizabeth Mugar Eveillard, the college's board chair, said the new policy affirms that Smith remains a women's college. "As we reflect on how Smith lives its values -- a commitment to access and diversity, to respecting the dignity of every individual, and to educating women for leadership across all realms of society -- we will be called, in changing times, to consider anew how we will choose to be a women's college," said McCartney and Eveillard.

Under Smith's new policy, applicants need only identify themselves as female on the Common Application to be eligible. In an interview, McCartney said that she was proud that Smith was adopting self-identification as the only method for determining female status -- a policy that has been advocated by transgender rights groups.

People who were born women but who identify as men will not be eligible for admission. But those who apply and are admitted as women and subsequently come to identify as men will be permitted to stay.

The college announced that it would continue to refer to all students as women. "In keeping with our tradition and identity as a college of and for women, Smith will continue to use gendered language, including female pronouns, in institutional communications," the statement said.

Smith has been a focus of transgender rights advocates since an incident in 2013 when a transgender woman said she was rejected by the college because of her gender identity. Smith disputed parts of the applicant's story, but the account prompted numerous protests and scrutiny for Smith. As one of the five Seven Sisters colleges that remain women's colleges, Smith's policies also attracted attention.

Since 2013, three other Seven Sisters colleges -- first Mount Holyoke College, and then Bryn Mawr and Wellesley Colleges -- have announced that they would admit transgender applicants. Barnard College is the remaining Seven Sisters women's college that has yet to change its policy, but the college announced in December that it was studying the issue.

In California, meanwhile, two women's colleges -- Mills and Scripps Colleges -- have also moved to admit transgender applicants.

At the colleges that have moved to admit transgender students, including Smith so far, the reaction from students and faculty members and many alumnae has been strongly positive. McCartney said in an interview that Smith officials had been watching social media and finding near universal praise.

A majority of women's colleges have yet to change their policies and some are explicit about that.

Hollins University, for example, outlines in its student handbook that if an undergraduate admitted as a woman "undergoes sex reassignment from female to male (as defined by the university below) at any point during her time at Hollins, the student will be helped to transfer to another institution since conferral of a Hollins degree will be limited to those who are women." The handbook goes on to define sex reassignment as "when an undergraduate student self-identifies as a male and initiates any of the following processes: 1) undergoes hormone therapy with the intent to transform anatomically from female to male; 2) undergoes any surgical process (procedure) to transform from female to male; or 3) changes her name legally with the intent of identifying herself as a man."

The policy also states that if an undergraduate "is a residential student and she chooses to begin sex reassignment as defined above, the administration reserves the right, based on the best interest of the student and the university community, to decide if the student will be permitted to continue living in university housing."

The Hollins policy does indicate that it may change in the future, saying: "Recognizing the changing landscape as it pertains to individuals on the transgender spectrum, this policy will be reviewed on a regular basis."

Advocates for transgender students believe the landscape has changed in such a way that more colleges are likely to follow Smith. "Yes, without a doubt we are at a tipping point," said Shane Windmeyer, executive director of Campus Pride, a group that advocates for gay, lesbian and transgender students.

He said he remains concerned that "most high-level administrators and staff have a steep learning curve to go with the newfound awareness on trans people... locked into a binary way of thinking about gender identity and a narrow way of viewing gender expression."

For women's colleges, the centrality of admissions to being inclusive of transgender students has been obvious, since the colleges use gender definitions to decide whom may be considered for admission. But Campus Pride has been involved in efforts at coeducational colleges as well, over the issue of collecting data (on admissions applications and elsewhere) about students' gender identity. For coeducational colleges, Campus Pride has urged colleges to add voluntary questions for applicants and those who enroll on sexual orientation and gender identity so that institutions can see whether they are attracting and retaining gay, lesbian and transgender students -- much the way colleges consider their performance at attracting and graduating minority students.

Some colleges -- such as Duke University -- have added such questions.

But many colleges rely on the Common Application, which in 2011 rejected the idea of adding voluntary questions about sexual orientation and gender identity. Smith's announcement referred to the Common Application and the need for applicants to check "female" on its form.

Windmeyer said that Smith's announcement is more evidence that the Common Application should reconsider its 2011 decision. "It was the wrong decision back then and it still is today," he said. "Things are changing. The Common App in order to be relevant will need to change."

A spokesperson for the Common Application did not respond to an email question on whether the organization was considering a change.

WHAT THE EXPERTS SAY

1. For colleges like Smith, whose identity is built upon the gender of its students, how might a strict definition of "woman" and "man" negatively impact female students who are cisgender (meaning they identify with the gender assigned to them at birth based on their biological sex)?

2. At a school like Hollins, should a student who was assigned female at birth but identifies as male be required to leave the school even if they do not undergo sex reassignment procedures? Why or why not?

"SOUTH MOUNTAIN COMMUNITY COLLEGE PUSHES TO CORRECT COURSE ON GRADUATION AND RETENTION RATES," BY SOPHIA KUNTHARA, FROM *CRONKITE NEWS*, DECEMBER 30, 2015

The call came two weeks before Joana Sotelo's birthday in February 2013: her brother had been deported to Mexico.

"When something emotional comes to your life, it just makes you want to work harder for what you want,"

Sotelo said. "It just gave me more of a reason to work toward my goals."

For Sotelo, a first-generation college student at South Mountain Community College, that goal was to obtain a college education and become an immigration lawyer. She wanted to attend Arizona State University after high school, but couldn't afford it.

Her mother works as a supervisor of housekeeping at the Paradise Valley Country Club and her father is a landscaper. Sotelo is the first of her five siblings to pursue a higher education.

A Presidential Honor scholarship made community college possible and Sotelo is on track to graduate in the spring before hopefully transferring to ASU to major in Justice Studies.

For Sotelo, SMCC was the first step.

SMCC, located at 7050 S. 24th St., serves some of the poorest areas of the Valley, including South Phoenix, Guadalupe and Laveen. In its zip code, 85042, only 22 percent of the population over 25 years old has a bachelor's degree or higher, according to census data. In its congressional district, District 7, about 35 percent of the people fall below the poverty line.

The college, opened at its current location in 1981, had slightly more than 4,000 students in the fall semester of 2015, 32 percent of them full-time students, 68 percent part-time.

"Here in this community, we don't really have access to schooling if it weren't for this school … built 30-something years ago," Sotelo said. "We didn't really have anything over here in this area. We don't have hospitals … we don't have schools."

"So I feel like it being built, it has been the first step to many, three generations now. It's been 30 years, and it will continue to be the first step to many first-generation students here."

But SMCC, like many community colleges around the nation, faces low retention and graduation rates. Only 29 percent of part-time students and 60 percent of the full-time students who enrolled at the college in Fall 2013 returned the next year.

Compared to the nine other colleges in the Maricopa County Community College district, SMCC ties for the fifth-lowest full time retention rate and the second-lowest part-time retention rate.

From the fall 2014 semester to fall 2015, the full-time headcount dropped by about 2.25 percent and the part-time headcount fell by about 5.9 percent.

The district, which includes 10 community colleges, a corporate college and two skill centers, operates as "a community of colleges — colleges for the community" to provide higher education to the diverse populations it serves, according to the district's strategic plan for 2013-2016.

Tuition also is significantly cheaper than at four-year universities; SMCC charged $84 per credit hour for Maricopa County residents during the spring 2014 semester.

Additionally, the district is aiming to increase the number of students obtaining their associate degrees and certificates or transferring to a university in Arizona by 50 percent by 2020. "Attaining this goal will contribute to Arizona's economic recovery as well as increase the quality of life for a more educated workforce," according to the district plan.

Without the college, there would be no other opportunity to achieve a higher education and increase the earning power for students like Sotelo.

"If it wasn't for the scholarship, I'd still be at home scraping dishes somewhere," she said.

When community colleges first began, the goal was to provide access to education, according to Callan Fay, a student success specialist at SMCC. But the focus has shifted by using data to identify students' strengths and help them identify career paths and study plans that play to their strengths and encourage them to finish their degree.

Nationally, retention rates for full and part-time students also have been problematic for community colleges.

Hana Lahr, a senior research assistant at the Center for Community College Research at Columbia University, said because community colleges don't have programs with set plans of study, students often take a variety of courses that do not lead to an end goal.

"The problem when it comes to retention is because they are disconnected, they're not set up to maximizing retention or completion," Lahr said. "When a student comes in, they're taking these courses, the programs aren't clearly laid out ... the programs of study aren't coherent, they're disconnected."

Some students have to take multiple remedial education classes as well, which can prolong their time in college.

But having doubts about what classes to take and what career path to pursue isn't limited to community colleges, said Osaro Ighodaro, the vice president of student development at SMCC. Ighodaro, who worked at ASU for years, said students starting college at a four-year university also struggle to stick to their study plan.

But more community college students are first-generation or non-traditional students from lower-income families.

"Because of the socio-economic status of the majority of our students, again you have the population in the university but less so than in community college, part of the challenge is students having to work two, three jobs to have an apartment, fend for their family and having to go to school," Ighodaro said.

Nationally, 44 percent of low-income students attend community college after high school, while only 15 percent of high-income students attend community college to start their higher education, according to the Community College Research Center's analysis of the Education Longitudinal Study.

Ighodaro noted that SMCC has some programs to help students whose education may be hindered by lack of financial support. A food pantry stocked by faculty, for example, is on campus for students who come to campus hungry. It's not funded by the college or district, but something faculty do to help the students.

Lower-income and many minority students also are less familiar with college environments and don't know about the resources available to them, she said.

"Being a first generation minority is tough, because when you need help with your homework and stuff, mom and dad can't help you," Sotelo said.

Sotelo works at the college's Learning Resource Center, where students come to study or for tutoring. She works at the front desk 15 hours a week as part of her work-study program.

For many students at the South Phoenix campus, this is not only their best shot at a college degree, it's their only shot.

Chasity Chase grew up on the Navajo reservation. Her father told her to focus on one thing: getting an education. With few opportunities near the reservation, Chase saw moving to the Valley as the only option, despite her lack of knowledge about life outside of the reservation.

She didn't even own a cell phone.

"He always stressed 'get an education, that's where you'll get the money, I don't want you struggling like the rest of the people moving from place to place with construction jobs,' " Chase said.

The mother of four, she moved to South Phoenix and enrolled at SMCC to pursue a career in psychology. SMCC was close to her South Phoenix home, affordable and had flexible classes. She was able to make money doing general labor at construction sites on the side, often doing the cleanup work.

She plans to return to the reservation when she's done.

"That's my motivation for that, just to go back home and educate people, more awareness for the outside world," Chase said.

Since Sotelo enrolled in SMCC, even her mother has expressed an interest taking classes.

"I think people don't think of doing something until they see it, they see other people doing it ... I didn't see my older brothers go to college, but I'm being the first person to go to college, Sotelo said.

"They (her younger brothers) are seeing me do it, so other people around this community are going to be like 'Hey, someone else did it. I can too.' "

1. Both community colleges and four-year programs cite retention as a problem and a lack of a plan of study affects students in both types of schools. What are some factors that may be common to students in both situations? What are some ways in which not having a set track of study might be advantageous to some students?

2. Community colleges usually have fewer steps in the application process to make enrollment accessible to as many students as possible. How might restricting some of the college's resources and classes to students who do not have a declared major affect retention? Would such limitations act as a deterrent for prospective students or encourage academic commitment? Why?

"WHILE RETHINKING ADMISSIONS PROCESS, CONSIDER CREATIVITY," BY JAMES C. KAUFMAN, FROM *THE CONVERSATION* WITH THE PARTNERSHIP OF THE UNIVERSITY OF CONNECTICUT, JANUARY 27, 2016

The Turning the Tide report released last week by the Harvard Graduate School of Education has colleges and

universities across the country taking a hard look at what
many believe is a deeply flawed admissions process.

A number of colleges have already been reexam-
ining their admissions process. In September last year,
more than 80 leading colleges and universities announced
the formation of the Coalition for Access, Affordability
and Success, so as to make changes in the admissions
process and diversify student bodies.

The new report characterizes the message being sent
by colleges to high schools "as simply valuing their achievements, not their responsibility for others and their communities." It asks college admissions officers to take the following
three primary steps to improve the admissions process so
that it is fairer and inculcates a concern for others:

- promote more meaningful contributions through community service and other engagement for the public good
- assess how students engage and contribute to family
  as well as community across race, culture and class
- redefine achievement in ways that level the playing
  field for economically diverse students and reduce
  excessive achievement pressure.

However, what often gets left out of admission
criteria is a student's creativity. As a creativity researcher,
I have studied many aspects of creativity that reinforce
the idea that creativity is a valuable and necessary attri-
bute for students in the 21st century.

WHY MEASURE CREATIVITY?

Creativity can be seen at all levels – from young children
to geniuses. Creativity can help us discover new things,
from the next generation of smartphones to new ways of
recycling our trash.

It enables us to make art, tell stories, design buildings, test hypotheses and try new recipes. Indeed, creative people have been found to be more likely to succeed in business and be happier in life.

There is a growing volume of research that shows putting greater emphasis on creativity assessments in the college application process could provide a more holistic impression of students' potential. Right now, we look only at a narrow range of abilities, which means that we over-reward people with certain strengths and penalize people with other strengths.

Studies have shown that the most widely used standardized performance tests for college admission, the SAT, is a better predictor of college success for white students than African-American and Hispanic-American students.

However, creativity assessments are more likely to be gender- and ethnically neutral, thereby avoiding the potential for bias.

A study we conducted recently on more than 600 college applicants compared applicants' performance on a series of online tests assessing various forms of creativity to application data, which included SAT scores, class rank and college admission interview scores.

We found that traditional admissions measures (SAT scores and GPA) were only weakly related to the creativity measures. Further, people with high creative self-efficacy (i.e., people who think they are creative) did slightly worse on some admission tests.

We are continuing to capture data about students over the course of their college careers to assess whether including creativity tests with traditional admissions measures can better predict student outcomes such as retention, college success and graduation rates.

ASSESSING CREATIVITY MAKES A DIFFERENCE

We do understand that assessing students' creativity would not be easy. But that is not to say it is impossible.

As part of the admissions process, students could be asked about how they would solve world problems or what their dream job would be or how they would spend lottery winnings; these responses could then be rated for their creativity by admission officers or trained raters. Many studies have shown that this is a reliable and valid way of measuring creativity, although it can be resource-intensive.

Some universities may ask such questions in current admissions, but most do not actually score answers for creativity. In fact, being creative on admissions essays can actually hurt students.

If there are concerns about adding too much stress on students during applications, schools could use a portfolio approach in which students could simply upload a poem, drawing, movie, invention or science experiment that they have already produced.

The fact is that using creativity as a criterion in admissions has been done before. At one point, Cornell University Professor of Human Development Robert Sternberg and colleagues included creativity and practical intelligence as an optional part of college admissions at Tufts University. What Sternberg and colleagues found was that students enjoyed the application process more and the average SAT score of all applicants increased from previous years.

In an equally important outcome, differences on these new measures showed reduced or no ethnic differences, and minority admissions increased.

Such results are typical in creativity studies. Whereas many standardized or intelligence tests show ethnic, cultural or gender differences, creativity measures tend to produce no differences – everyone has the same potential to be creative.

Creativity is more important than ever as college and universities try to both emphasize diversity in their student population and seek future innovators in science, technology, engineering and math, otherwise known as the STEM fields. Including creativity helps accomplish both goals.

If early impressions of the Turning the Tide report are any indication, we could be heading into a pivotal time for college admissions. Such changes should not be limited to the scope of this landmark report. We need to be creative.

1. The author states that standardized test scores predict students' proficiency differently for white students than for African American or Hispanic American students. But tests like the SAT and ACT are still used to represent academic standards. How might a student from such a background prepare themselves for an admissions process that re-emphasizes creativity?

CHAPTER 2

WHAT THE GOVERNMENT AND POLITICIANS SAY

Ensuring that students continue on to college is an important way to help strengthen the economy, keep the United States on the cutting edge in areas like science, and make sure that young people have the skills they need to succeed. Because of this, it is crucial for the government at the local, state, and federal levels to craft policies that make sure students are given the best possible chance at getting into colleges and universities, and to hold institutions accountable when they do not meet their responsibilities to students. With the future of the country at stake, making sure that the government is addressing education in a meaningful and reasonable way is extremely important. But there is a great deal of debate about how policy can best confront the challenges of higher education.

FROM "REMARKS BY THE PRESIDENT ON EDUCATION," BY PRESIDENT BARACK OBAMA, FROM THE WHITE HOUSE ARCHIVES, OCTOBER 17, 2016

So, by now you've settled into the new year. Right? Adjusted to classes. You're preparing for Spirit Week. (Applause.) Learning how to ballroom dance. (Laughter.) I remember having to do that. Getting the nerve to text that cute girl or boy in your English class. (Laughter.) I don't remember that; we did not have texts. We had to send little notes. And then we used to actually have to go up to somebody if we liked them and talk to them. So that may happen to you someday. (Laughter.) Seniors are looking at colleges, taking tests, filling out all the forms. (Applause.) Malia just went through this, so I know how tough this is for you and for the parents.

But as I'm winding down my presidency -- I was so impressed with Banneker the last time I was here in 2011 that I wanted to come back -- (applause) -- because you're an example of a school that's doing things the right way. And I believe that if you're going to be able to do whatever you want to do in your lives -- if you want to become a teacher, or a doctor, or start a business, or develop the next great app, or be President -- then you've got to have great education.

We live in a global economy. And when you graduate, you're no longer going to be competing just with somebody here in D.C. for a great job. You're competing with somebody on the other side of the world, in China or in India, because jobs can go wherever they want because of the Internet and because of technology. And the best jobs are going to go to the people who are the best educated -- whether in India or China, or anywhere in the world.

So when I took office almost eight years ago, we knew that our education system was falling short when it came to preparing young people like you for that reality. Our public schools had been the envy of the world, but the world caught up. And we started getting outpaced when it came to math and science education. And African American and Latino students, in part because of the legacy of discrimination, too often lagged behind our white classmates -- something called the achievement gap that, by one estimate, costs us hundreds of billions of dollars a year. And we were behind other developed countries when it came to the number of young people who were getting a higher education. So I said, when I first came into office, by 2020 I want us to be number one again. I want us to be number one across the board.

So we got to work, making real changes to improve the chances for all of our young people, from the time they're born all the way through until they got a career. And the good news is that we've made real progress. So I just wanted to talk to you about the progress we've made, because you are the reason we've made progress -- some outstanding young people all across the country.

We recently learned that America's high school graduation rate went up to 83 percent, which is the highest on record. That's good news. (Applause.) More African American and Latino students are graduating than ever before. (Applause.) Right here in D.C., in just five years, the graduation rate in the District of Columbia public schools went from just 53 percent to 69 percent. (Applause.) So

D.C.'s graduation rates grew faster than any other place in the country this year -- this past year. That's something to be really proud of. (Applause.)

Now, of course, here at Banneker, you graduated 100 percent of your seniors last year. (Applause.) One hundred percent. It's been a while since I did math, but 100 percent is good. (Laughter.) You can't do better than that. So what all these numbers mean is that more schools across D.C. and across the country are starting to catch up to what you guys are doing here, at this school.

Now, some of the changes we made were hard, and some of them were controversial. We expected more from our teachers and our students. But the hard work that people have put in across the country has started to pay off.

And I just want to talk to you a little bit about some of the things that we did. It starts with our youngest learners. High-quality early education is one of the best investments we can make, which is why we've added over 60,000 children to Head Start. We called for high-quality preschool for every four-year-old in America. And when I took office, only 38 states offered access to state-funded preschool. Today, it's up to 46. We're trying to get those last holdouts to do the right thing. And, by the way, the District of Columbia leads the nation with the highest share of children -- nearly 9 out of 10 -- in high-quality preschool. And that's a big achievement. (Applause.)

We launched then a competition called Race to the Top, which inspired states to set higher, better standards so that we could out-teach and out-compete other nations, and make sure that we've got high expectations for our students. D.C. was one of the winners of this competition.

It upgraded standards, upgraded curriculum, worked to help teachers build their skills. And that, in part, is why D.C. has done so well.

We realized that in today's world, when you all have a computer in your pocket in those phones, then you need to learn not just how to use a phone, you need to learn computer science. So we're working with private and philanthropic partners to bring high schools into the 21st century and give you a more personalized and real-world experience. We're bringing in high-speed internet into schools and libraries, reaching 20 million more students and helping teachers with digital learning. And coding isn't, by the way, just for boys in Silicon Valley, so we're investing more in getting girls and young women and young people of color and low-income students into science and engineering and technology and math. (Applause.)

And because we know that nothing is more important than a great teacher -- and you've got some great teachers here, as well as a great principal at Banneker -- (applause) -- we have focused on preparing and developing and supporting and rewarding excellent educators. You all know how hard they work. They stay up late grading your assignments. That's why you got all those marks all over your papers. They pull sometimes money out of their own pockets to make that lesson extra special. And I promise you, the teachers here and the teachers around the country, they're not doing it for the pay -- because teachers, unfortunately, still aren't paid as much as they should be. They're not doing it for the glory. They're doing it because they love you, and they believe in you, and they want to help you succeed. So teachers deserve more than just our gratitude --

they deserve our full support. And we've got to make their lives easier, which is why we enacted a law to fix No Child Left Behind, which gives teachers more flexibility to spend more time teaching creatively than just spending all their time teaching to a test. Give your teachers a big round of applause. (Applause.) They deserve it.

So we've made real progress, but here's the thing -- and I think all of you know this because you go to this great school -- a high school education these days is not enough. By 2020, two out of three job openings require some form of higher education. Now, that doesn't always mean a four-year college degree, but it does mean -- whether it's a four-year university, or a community college, or some sort of training program -- you've got to get a little bit more than just what you're getting in high school.

It used to be that a high school job might be enough because you could go into a factory or even go into an office and just do some repetitive work, and if you were willing to work hard you could make a decent living. But the problem is repetitive work now is done by machines. And that's just going to be more and more true. So in order for you to succeed in the marketplace, you've got to be able to think creatively; you've got to be able to work with a team; you've got to be able to work with a machine and figure out how to make it tailored for the specific require-ments of your business and your job. All those things require some more sophisticated thinking than just sitting there and just doing the same thing over and over again. And that's why you've got to have more than just a high school education.

And if you doubt that, I just want to give you some statistics. Compared to a high school diploma, just getting a degree from a two-year school, going to a community college and getting an associate's degree could earn you more than $300,000 over the course of your lifetime. And a four-year degree earns you a million dollars more than if you just had a high school degree. Think about that. A million dollars -- that's real money.

So one of the things that we're trying to do is to make it easier for you to access free money for college -- to figure out how you can pay for your college without having a mountain of debt. And the key thing, as you know here at Banneker, but I want all the students around the country to do this -- and Michelle and I and others have been really emphasizing this -- is to fill out your FAFSA, the Free Application for Federal Student Aid.

How many people -- how many seniors here have already filled out their FAFSA forms? (Applause.) All right. How many seniors here have not filled out their FAFSA forms? Fess up now. (Laughter.) You sure? All right, I just want to make sure now. And, juniors, you can start getting ready now.

Because what the FAFSA does is it puts you in the running for scholarships, grants, loans, work-study jobs, all to help you pay for college. And we've made it simpler than ever. And it's available right now at FAFSA.gov -- FAFSA. gov. And since this is one of the most important investments of your life, next year's FAFSA is also going to direct you to something we created, called our College Scorecard.

Now, here's what this is. It gives you comprehensive information on every college in America. Now, some of you who have started applying for colleges, you know about these college rankings, right? It's like, oh, this is the best school. And some of that information is useful;

some of it not so much. But unlike traditional rankings that focus on which school has the fanciest dorm or the nicest football stadiums, or is the most expensive or the most exclusive, what our College Scorecard does is it focuses on some of the things that really matter for your future. Things like how many students actually graduate from the school -- because it's not enough just to enroll in college; you've got to graduate from college. How much money do their alumni earn? What percentage of their students can pay back their loans? And what we've done is we've worked with companies like Google to put this information right at your fingertips.

So for a decision this important, we want you to be able to comparison shop to figure out how do you get the best value for your money, just like if you were buying something on Amazon. If you were buying a car or you're buying a phone or you're buying anything, especially if it's a pretty big purchase, you want to know ahead of time, is this legit. And what this does is makes you think about what your options are.

Now, you've got some great counselors here. Obviously, you should work with them. But not every student may be going to a school like Banneker that has as many good counselors to think about their college education. And using this College Scorecard is going to be helpful for them to do a little comparison shopping. Because you don't want to go to the school just because it's the closest one, and it turns out it's more expensive and doesn't do as good of a job as if you were willing to maybe travel someplace else, and it turns out that you could get the financial aid you need to go to a school that's more suited toward your needs.

So we also reformed, by the way, the student loan system. When I came into office, you had tens of billions of dollars that were going to big banks, serving as middlemen for your student loans. We said, well, let's cut out the banks. Let's give the money directly to the students so they can afford college and we can make the loans cheaper, and we can expand Pell grants.

And now, what we're trying to do is to push to make two years of community college free for every responsible student all across the country. All across the country. (Applause.) And we're starting to work with colleges and universities around the country to bring down the cost of college so that at the end of four years of college you're not saddled with a whole bunch of debt -- because nobody should be priced out of a higher education. (Applause.)

So bottom line is: higher graduation rates, higher college attendance rates, more money for Pell grants and work to make sure that the interest rate on student loans haven't gone up; working to expand early childhood education and preschool; continuing to watch and work with states as they try to implement reforms to make K-12 better; holding colleges more accountable for giving information so that students can make good decisions. We've made a lot of progress. We have made a lot of progress in terms of making sure that young people across the country get the kind of great education that you're getting here at Banneker. And I am really proud of what we've accomplished. I'm proud of what the District of Columbia has accomplished.

But I just want to be honest with you: We've still got more work to do. So as I go, I'm giving you kind of a final report card, transcript on what more we've got to get done.

There are still too many states that are cutting back on public education. And part of the reason tuition is going up is because states aren't putting as much money into state education, universities, community colleges as they used to. That's why, if you're 18, by the way, you've got to vote to make sure that the folks who represent you actually deliver. (Applause.)

We've still got too many states that have not really worked in a serious way to raise standards and improve performance. In too many school districts, we still have schools that, despite the heroic efforts of a lot of great teachers, are not fully preparing our kids for success because they just don't have the resources to do it or the structure to do it. We've still got too many high schools where a third of their students do not earn their diplomas on time.

For too many students in America, zip code still determines how far they'll go. And that's not acceptable. Some of you probably have friends or family who are just as smart or talented or as capable as you, but they didn't have the same support or the right opportunities or didn't get in the right school, and so now don't have the same shot at success. Am I right? Because I know that's true in our family. Michelle and I, we've got cousins and friends who we've known since they were shorties, little kids -- (laughter) -- and they -- we know how smart they are because they were just as smart as we were, but just the luck of the draw was they didn't get the same chance as we did. And that's not right.

So that's why I started something called My Brother's Keeper initiative, because what we want to do is help more young people, especially kids of color, get mentorships and the resources and the guidance they need to succeed. And I'm going to stay involved with that even after I'm done being President. (Applause.) Because we all have a part to play in making sure every single child has every single opportunity to achieve his or her dreams.

That's what Banneker is all about. That's what you can see in somebody like Ifunaya. I mean, that's an incredible young lady who's going to succeed because she has an incredible school in addition to an incredible family. (Applause.) And so we're so proud of her.

There's another person I want to just call out -- Amari McDuffie. Where's Amari? Where's Amari? There she is right there, right in front. (Applause.) So, hey, Amari. I'm going to talk about you for a second. (Laughter.)

So Amari was born with a heart and a lung condition. And sometimes she had to miss a lot of school because of her illness. And you know, Banneker is a pretty rigorous school, so she was worried about staying on top of her work. But everybody in this family rallied around her and made sure she was keeping up. Her history teacher, Mr. Goldfarb -- where's Mr. Goldfarb? (Applause.) Is he here or did he cut assembly? (Laughter.) So Mr. Goldfarb came to visit her when Amari was in the hospital for weeks, brought a card from the whole class. And so Amari, she was talking about the support everybody here gave her, and she said, "I believed in myself because my teachers believed in me."

And that's the kind of community that we want in every school -- where you're looking out for each other and you're taking care of one another. And so now Amari plans to be a doctor so she can help kids who had illnesses like hers. And that's what's possible

-- (applause) -- that's what's possible when we're all committed to each other's success; when we understand that no matter what you look like, where you come from, what faith you are, whether you're a boy or a girl -- that you should have great opportunities to succeed. And that requires you to put effort into it.

Michelle and I talk a lot because we travel around the world and sometimes we forget that there are places around the world where people have so little but the kids are so hungry for an education. And they don't even have an actual roof over their head in some of their schools. And so even if you're really poor in this country, you can succeed if you want to invest in the teachers and the community, and everybody raises standards and believes in each other. And that's what we want all of America to believe, in every kid -- because there's magic in each and every one of you. And we just have to help you unleash it and nurture it and realize it.

And, by the way, it's because of young people like you that I leave the presidency never more optimistic than I am right now, because I've met so many young people around the country whose energy, and excitement, and how you treat each other, with respect. That gives me a lot of confidence, a lot of faith for our country.

So I know you guys are going to keep on working hard. You're going to keep making our communities proud. If us adults do our part and we stay focused on making sure every school is as great as this one, and that every young person has those same opportunities, and everybody has a teacher like Mr. Goldfarb looking out for them, I've got no doubt that we're going to continue to build a country where everybody has the chance to make of their lives what they will. And that's what America is all about. All right. Proud of you, Bulldogs. Thank you. God bless you. God bless the United States of America. Fill out those FAFSA forms! Thank you. (Applause.)

1. What has the District of Columbia done to increase college admissions rates? How can federal and local partnerships increase college enrollment?

2. According to President Obama, how does higher education shape the country?

"GOVERNOR CUOMO ANNOUNCES $3.2 MILLION TO PROMOTE COLLEGE ACCESS TO LOW INCOME STUDENTS," FROM THE NEW YORK STATE GOVERNOR'S OFFICE, DECEMBER 8, 2014

Governor Andrew M. Cuomo today announced $3.2 million in federal College Access Challenge Grant Program funding has been awarded to 20 organizations across the State to help increase college enrollment and directly serve low-income students. This funding comes from a $6.2 million grant awarded to the State in 2013 by the U.S. Department of Education and will be administered by the New York State Higher Education Services Corporation. A $6.5 million grant was also awarded in 2014 and will be used to support college access services and activities for the 2015-16 school year.

"Increasing access to higher education for all New Yorkers is a top priority of this administration, and this funding will help put more lower income students on track for a college career," Governor Cuomo said. "Working with our partners in government, we will continue to invest in our home-grown talent to provide students with the education they deserve."

The funding from the College Access Grant Challenge Program will support strategies for student success through five projects implemented at specific organizations across the State:

Providing college-ready, low-income students with customized information and assistance throughout the college application process, and match students to colleges that best align with their academic potential. Award recipients for this project are:

- Syracuse University, Syracuse, NY - $49,988
- New York City Outward Bound Center, Inc., LIC, NY - $183,772
- Henry Street Settlement, New York, NY - $85,000

Facilitating FAFSA completion to help low-income students access financial aid. Award recipients for this project are:

- New Settlement Apartments (The Crenulated Company, Ltd.) Bronx, NY - $124,740
- Veterans Outreach Center, Inc., Rochester - NY $72,980
- D'Youville College, Buffalo, NY - $72,898
- YMCA of Greater New York, New York, NY- $136,860

Providing intensive college preparation, enrollment and persistence counseling, coaching and direction on the transition to college beginning in middle school through the end of freshman year of college. Award recipients for this project are:

- Cypress Hills Local Development Corporation, Brooklyn, NY - $75,000
- Yonkers Partners in Education, Yonkers, NY - $492,489
- Long Island University – Brooklyn, Greenvale, NY - $49,680
- Sports and Arts in Schools Foundation, Queens, NY - $49,680
- Kingsbridge Heights Community Center, Bronx, NY - $162,535
- Good Shepherd Services, New York, NY - $213,900
- Harlem Center for Education, Inc., New York, NY - $74,897
- Sunnyside Community Services, Sunnyside, NY - $109,179
- Bottom Line, Inc., Brooklyn, NY - $200,000
- SUNY College at Farmingdale, Farmingdale, NY - $270,000

Reconnecting adult learners to postsecondary education opportunities through services that increase their college completion rates and reduce time to complete their degrees. Award recipients for this project are:

- Trinity Alliance of the Capital Region, Albany, NY - $270,941
- Orange County Community College – SUNY, Middletown, NY - $53,630

Establishing new and creative uses of technology to increase college opportunities for low-income students. The award recipient for this project is:

- Excelsior College, Albany, NY - $449,439

Details about the College Access Innovation Grants can be found at HESC.ny.gov/CACG.

"Through these college access grants, New York has been able to work in partnership with exceptional community-based organizations to provide low-income students with the tools and motivation to plan for, apply to and graduate from college," said Elsa Magee, Acting President of HESC. "Over the past 6 years, New York State has successfully applied for six awards totaling $35.5 million, which has allowed us to continue to support students in their communities. We're pleased to be able to continue that support through the program's final year."

Congressman Charles B. Rangel said, "I thank Governor Cuomo for his unyielding commitment to opening doors for students in our community to gain access to higher education. Ensuring college access is the greatest investment we can make to help them succeed. In Congress I will keep fighting for legislative efforts to make college affordable to everyone in our great State and Nation."

Congresswoman Louise Slaughter said, "A person's income should never limit their potential or access to higher education, especially if that person is a veteran of the U.S. military. I am glad that we are undertaking a comprehensive effort to make college more affordable, and especially thankful that the Veterans Outreach Center will be able to help local veterans access a college education. As chairwoman of the House Rules Committee in 2009, I was proud to bring the Post-9/11 GI bill — legislation that expanded opportunities for Iraq and Afghanistan veterans to go to college — to the House floor for a vote. We must continue to support our veterans and invest in accessible higher education, just as this grant does."

Congressman Eliot Engel said, "College graduates generally earn more than those who only have a high school diploma, but higher education is still a distant dream for far too many low-income students. These federal funds will help make college more accessible by giving students the guidance they need to navigate the financial aid process and better prepare for college. Yonkers Partners in Education has worked hard to provide these types of services, and I am pleased that they are among the recipients."

Congressman José E. Serrano said, "Oftentimes, promising students from disadvantaged backgrounds can't reach the next academic level simply because they don't have access to the information, counseling, and resources they need to apply to college. We have to invest in these students to help them reach their full potential. The funds announced today by Governor Cuomo will help thousands of New York City students, including students from the Bronx, access greater academic opportunities and successfully graduate from college."

Congressman Jerrold Nadler said, "Many deserving students are unable to attend college simply because they cannot afford the rising costs. I am pleased my district has been selected to receive a CACG grant so that low–income New Yorkers will have the support to start down the pathway to success. These grants strengthen our community and the city as a whole. New York ought to be a place where good students, no matter their income, can afford to go to college. Those who aspire to the highest levels of education are vital to enriching our world, and we should do all we can to empower them."

Congresswoman Carolyn B. Maloney said, "I want to thank Governor Cuomo for taking a bold step to help young people afford higher education. A college education is the gateway to better opportunities in life. This much-needed funding will help thousands of low-income and at risk students who might otherwise be unable to gain access to the halls of higher learning. Applying to college can be daunting without someone to help guide you. With these newly allocated funds the state is taking steps towards demystifying the process so that everyone has a fair shot at improving their future."

Congresswoman Nydia M. Velázquez said, "Tuition and college costs can be a significant hurdle for working families and young people seeking a college education. I am pleased to see these federal resources go to community-based organizations that are dedicated to helping more New Yorkers overcome financial barriers and obtain a college degree."

Congressman Joe Crowley said, "Making college more accessible is fundamental to closing the opportunity gap that exists for our low-income communities. At a time when rising tuition costs are hindering our youth from pursuing higher education, these federal grants will go a long way toward making sure students are not only taking advantage of any financial assistance available to them but that they are also adequately prepared for college entry. An investment in education is an investment in our future and I thank Governor Cuomo and the New York State Higher Education Services Corporation for making sure these support programs are there for those who need them."

Congressman Brian Higgins said, "Financial barriers should never dictate whether or not a student can pursue higher education. Western New York is home to some of the best colleges and technical schools in the nation, attracting students from around the world. It is important that we provide as many resources as possible to first generation and low income students to receive the financial assistance to apply, attend, and advance at these institutions."

Congressman Paul Tonko said, "To secure economic prosperity for future generations, college must be an opportunity to all Americans, instead of just accessible to a privileged few. Here in the Capital Region and across the nation, institutions like Excelsior College and Trinity Alliance execute phenomenal programs that develop our communities and prepare New Yorkers for the next step in their careers – but they need our support. I thank Governor Cuomo for recognizing that quality and affordable access to higher education is the key to a happy and successful life maintaining a well-trained workforce in nationwide."

Congressman Sean Patrick Maloney said, "Each and every New Yorker deserves the opportunity to further their education and achieve the American dream. This investment for SUNY Orange removes barriers to a college education that stop too many adults from achieving a college education, while growing our middle class and boosting our economy."

About HESC: HESC is New York State's student financial aid agency that helps people pay for college and a national leader in providing need based grant and scholarship award money to college-going students. At HESC's core are programs like the Tuition Assistance Program (TAP), numerous state scholarships, federal college access grants and a highly successful College Savings program. HESC puts college within the reach of hundreds of thousands of New Yorkers each year through programs like these and through the guidance it provides to students, families and counselors. In 2013-14, HESC helped more than 388,000 students achieve their college dreams by providing more than $984 million in grants, scholarships and loan forgiveness benefits, including $935.5 million awarded through the Tuition Assistance Program (TAP).

1. Why does Governor Cuomo want to make sure low-income students have access to funding for higher education?

2. Based on representatives' responses to the new measures, do you think this program will help or hurt students?

"GOVERNOR VETOES SB 2043" BY GOVERNOR BRUCE RAUNER, FROM THE OFFICE OF THE GOVERNOR OF THE STATE OF ILLINOIS, FEBRUARY 19, 2016

To the Honorable Members of The Illinois Senate, 99th General Assembly:

Today I veto Senate Bill 2043 from the 99th General Assembly, which would explode the State's budget deficit, exacerbate the State's cash flow crisis, and place further strain on social service providers and recipients who are already suffering from the State's deficit spending.

SB 2043 WOULD EXACERBATE OUR BUDGET AND CASH FLOW DEFICITS

Senate Bill 2043 would appropriate $721 million for the Monetary Award Program (MAP) and community colleges programs. Senate Bill 2043 proposes the same funding levels for these programs as were included in the unconstitutional, unbalanced budget passed by the General Assembly last year, which was opposed by many legislators, including Democrats, and which I vetoed.

Despite its constitutional obligation to balance the budget, the General Assembly has not put forward a plan to pay for these programs, whether through spending reductions, revenue, or cost-saving reforms. The Governor's Office of Management and Budget concluded that Senate Bill 2043 would add $721 million to the State's budget deficit.

Today, the Comptroller reports 48,000 vendor vouchers waiting to be paid, a $7.2 billion backlog of bills, and a grand total balance of $145 million in the general funds. This bill would spend money the State does not have.

Moreover, Senate Bill 2043's unfunded spending would significantly exacerbate the State's current cash flow challenges. To protect and prioritize General State Aid payments, the Comptroller would be forced to further delay payments for other goods and services across State government, putting social services further at risk. We have already seen that the State's deficit spending is harshest to social service providers and our State's most vulnerable residents. Senate Bill 2043 would further delay those payments at a time when those recipients are already under fiscal stress.

A BETTER, CONSTITUTIONAL WAY TO FUND HIGHER EDUCATION

The Constitution and our obligation to taxpayers require a balanced budget. Recognizing this, legislators in both the House of Representatives and the Senate put forward a plan to pay for higher education spending – not just those programs included in Senate Bill 2043, but also funding for our public universities. I thank them for their leadership.

House Bill 4539 and Senate Bill 2349 would appropriate $1.6 billion for higher education programs, while Senate Bill 2789 would authorize the Governor, Comptroller, and Treasurer to identify and implement funding by reallocating funds and reducing spending in other areas. Together these bills would fund MAP, community college programs, and our public universities, without exploding the deficit or exacerbating the State's cash flow crisis. This is a far more fiscally responsible – and constitutional – plan for funding higher education.

Therefore, pursuant to Section 9(b) of Article IV of the Illinois Constitution of 1970, I hereby return Senate Bill 2043, entitled "AN ACT concerning appropriations", with the foregoing objections, vetoed in its entirety.

Sincerely,
Bruce Rauner
GOVERNOR

1. Why did Governor Rauner veto this bill? What do his reasons tell you about how funding decisions are made?

2. What could Illinois do to help students meet the cost of college?

"LETTER TO THE HONORABLE BRUCE RAUNER, GOVERNOR OF ILLINOIS," BY MEMBERS OF CONGRESS BILL FOSTER, BOBBY RUSH, ROBIN L. KELLY, DANNY K. DAVIS, JAN SHCAKOWSKY, LUIS V. GUTIERREZ, MIKE QUIGLEY, CHERI BUSTOS, AND TAMMY DUCKWORTH, APRIL 11, 2016

Dear Governor Rauner,

We write to express our dismay over the plight of students in our state. As you may know, because of the prolonged budget impasse many Illinois colleges and universities have been scrambling to solve growing budget shortfalls. This has led to extreme measures, directly preventing our citizens from bettering their situation through education. Recent events at Chicago State University and the Illinois Institute of Technology exemplify these extreme measures and highlight a crisis that we urge you to use your authority to resolve.

This week, Chicago State announced preparations for massive layoffs starting April 30. They have sent notices of potential termination to all 900 of their employees, including 300 faculty members. A pillar of the Chicago's South Side, Chicago State is in danger of no longer being able to offer students a quality education at an affordable price. The Illinois Institute of Technology was recently forced to announce that students will need to pay back the grants they received through the Monetary Assistance Program this fall and a suspension of all assistance for the spring. Students are now being forced to choose between paying their grant money back immediately, accepting a 12 month loan at 6.8 percent interest or being denied from class registration, effectively forcing them to drop out.

In February, you vetoed a bill that could have helped solve this problem, publicly stating that this is "a very tragic situation" and "a failure of the government." As the Governor of our state, you have the responsibility to rectify these tragic situations and ensure that government operates properly.

"Students should not be made to suffer because of politics," Congressman Foster said. "The education of our young people is too important to the future of Illinois to be used as political leverage. It's time for the Governor to act."

We implore you to consider how funding education will improve our shared prospects and increase future revenue. Making the right choices now will have long term benefits. This issue is too important to our future to do nothing.

We urge you to reconsider your veto and become a part of the solution to this problem.

1. What are some of the concerns representatives raised with Governor Rauner? What are their suggestions for alternatives?

2. How can local and state governments work together to ensure students have access to higher education?

"PATCHWORK OF STATE LAWS AFFECTS UNDOCUMENTED STUDENTS," BY ROSEMARY LIVERSEDGE, FROM *NEWS21*, AUGUST 2010

PHOENIX — Lilly is not officially an American, but she feels like one. She was 4 years old when her mother brought her into the United States illegally.

"I'm 22 years old. I've been here all of my life. My friends are here. My life is here," Lilly said. "I love the U.S. more than anything."

Lilly spent her entire educational life just like a lot of other kids in Arizona schools — from learning the ABC's in kindergarten to joining the cheerleading team in high school.

She was a good student, joining the Achieving a College Education program, designed by Maricopa Community Colleges for students who are the first members of their families to seek a college education. Through the ACE program, Lilly earned college credit while still in high school.

Lilly graduated from Phoenix's Carl Hayden High School in 2006. The next year she began taking courses at her local community college. Her goal was to become a neonatologist — a doctor who cares for newborns.

But Lilly soon hit a roadblock. In 2006, the same year Lilly graduated from high school, Arizona voters approved Proposition 300, which made it illegal for undocumented students to receive state-funded financial aid or reduced in-state tuition rates.

During the 2006-2007 school year the in-state tuition rate for Maricopa County's community colleges was $65 per credit hour. A full time, in-state student could expect to pay around $1,500 per year. The out-of-state tuition rate was $280 per credit hour, with yearly tuition around $6,700.

Having to pay out-of-state rates for courses and receiving no financial aid, Lilly was able to hang on for a year with the help from her family. Her mother, at the time a house cleaner, took on extra work and each member of the family pooled their money to help with tuition.

But in the end it was not enough, and Lilly dropped out of college to work and help with family expenses. She felt her hard work in high school and the state's investment in her education was wasted.

"All these taxpayers have already paid for my education," Lilly said. "They paid for me to go to school. … So, basically I just need to go to college so I can pay back and I can provide as well, but I can't — not yet."

Lilly's problem is shared by undocumented students nationwide. Around 65,000 undocumented students who have lived in the U.S. for five years or longer graduate from high school each year. Depending on where they live, they can face either an easy or difficult path to a college education. If they do make it through college, they face a daunting challenge in finding good employment, because they're not legally eligible to work in the United States.

As some states are opening pathways to affordable college for undocumented students, others are clamping down. Meanwhile, Congress continues to debate the DREAM Act, a bill that would offer a path to citizenship for undocumented students who have lived in the country for a long time.

A PATCHWORK OF LAWS

Nine states that have passed laws that allow undocumented high school graduates to receive in-state tuition rates. They are California, New Mexico, Kansas, Nebraska, Illinois, New York, Texas, Utah and Washington. Both New Mexico and Texas also offer state financial aid to the undocumented.

Arizona, Oklahoma, Georgia and South Carolina have passed laws to prevent undocumented students from receiving in-state tuition and state financial aid.

Most states have no specific laws pertaining to undocumented students. In those states all students, including illegal immigrants, follow established rules for proving residency in the state in order to receive discounted tuition or state financial aid.

Federal financial aid is only offered to legal residents.

Jose Luis, an education major at Texas A&M University, is happy to be a Texan. Jose came to the United States with his family on a temporary visa when he was 14 years old. He began attending public schools and became the first in his family to graduate from high school. Thanks to a 2005 state law known as SB 1528, Jose was able to afford college. The law allows all high school graduates in Texas — as well as international students — to receive in-state tuition and state financial aid.

"I am very proud and thankful to God for blessing me to live in Texas where to some extent I can pursue my dream which is college. I will be the first one in my family to graduate from college," Jose Luis said. "I am very blessed to be able to go to college and I am thankful to this state that has SB 1528 because it gives me hope."

STATE VERSUS FEDERAL GOVERNMENT

As the number of illegal immigrant children in the United States has risen over the years, lawmakers and judges have faced questions about how to deal with educating them. Under the 1982 Supreme Court Decision in *Plyler v. Doe* all children must be offered access to a K-12 education.

As with other immigration issues, there is ongoing over the role of the federal government in deciding the fate of undocumented students.

The 1996 Illegal Immigration Reform and Responsibility Act addressed several areas regarding illegal immigration from border control to higher education.

Section 1623 of the act states "[A]n alien who is not lawfully present in the United States shall not be eligible on the basis of residence within a state (or a political subdivision) for any postsecondary education benefit unless a citizen or national of the United States is eligible for such a benefit."

Lawmakers, activists, and government officials attempting to understand the law have often come to one of two opposite conclusions.

One interpretation of the law says undocumented students should not be allowed to get in-state tuition and state financial aid because it gives them an advantage not available to other legal U.S. residents — those who may have to pay out-of-state tuition, or who were denied admission to college on academic grounds.

The other main interpretation is that undocumented students should be allowed to receive in-state tuition and state financial aid because they are not receiving any benefit that is not generally available to those who qualify.

Lawmakers nationwide have debated whether this federal law supersedes state laws on providing aid or in-state tuition to undocumented immigrants. But even if federal law is considered supreme on this issue, confusion still remains because of differing interpretations.

THE VALUE OF AN EDUCATION

Silvia Rodriguez says states that make it harder for illegal immigrants to get an education will pay a price for denying education to people who want it.

Rodriguez is a graduate student at Harvard University and an alumnus of Arizona State University. She is an undocumented immigrant whose family brought her to the United States at the age of 2. Rodriguez graduated from Phoenix's North High School in 2005 and worked her way through college in spite of the fact that she could not receive in-state tuition or state financial aid.

"There is a bigger problem," Rodriguez said. "Denying people an education doesn't make people want to return to their country of origin, so what's going to happen when those students turn 30 or 40 and don't have an education?"

That is a question addressed in a 2009 study by the RAND Corp., a top research lab, for the U.S. government. It said higher education levels among members of a community result in more tax dollars in government coffers, less use of welfare programs and fewer people in jail.

The study looked at a limited amount of data on immigrants but concluded: "The limited research we conducted regarding the effects of increasing immigrants' education on the public budget suggests that increases in an immigrant's education will also yield significant benefits to taxpayers."

But Arizona State Treasurer Dean Martin argues that illegal immigrants in the education system cost states millions of dollars up front. That's why as a state senator he authored Proposition 300, a ballot initiative that passed in 2006 requiring all students to prove their legal residency in order to be eligible for in-state tuition and state financial aid. It is the law that Lilly says ended her college career.

Martin says the issue is a matter of fairness and economics.

"Arizona is on the front lines literally for illegal immigration, and it's been a very expensive problem for the state," he said.

Beyond finances, Martin said under previous state laws U.S. citizens were being denied benefits that were available to illegal immigrants.

"The state was literally subsidizing illegal immigration," Martin said, "providing subsidies that legal U.S. residents from other states couldn't get or that legal citizens of Arizona were on waiting lists and could not get, while someone who was here illegally was able to get it. And that doesn't make any sense."

Martin said the state has tracked about $15 million in savings per year because the state's universities are required to keep track of the number of students who tried to get in-state tuition but were denied because of their immigration status. He estimates another $5 million per year may have been saved from those who never applied because they knew they would not qualify.

WHO PAYS FOR EDUCATION?

Government officials and economists differ on whether illegal immigrants actually pay for services they use, such as education.

Those against giving aid and discounted tuition rates to the undocumented say those students or their parents have not paid their share in taxes that help fund education because many receive their pay "under the table" skirting the requirement to pay taxes. They also argue that low-paid immigrant workers get tax breaks, just like other low-paid Americans, and are therefore a drain on the system.

Proponents of giving aid and in-state tuition to the undocumented argue that illegal immigrants do pay their way — through sales tax, property tax, payroll tax and some income tax, pointing out that even those immigrants who use false Social Security Numbers to gain work have taxes deducted from their paychecks. Proponents also argue that businesses gain from immigrant-provided cheap labor, which boosts the economy.

It can be difficult to track exactly which taxes pay for a students' education in public schools since the funding is usually a combination of money from tuition and fees, combined with local, state and federal tax dollars and some grants from private organizations.

In 2007, the nonpartisan Congressional Budget Office reviewed 29 studies on the topic of immigrants and taxes and concluded that the taxes immigrants pay were not enough to offset the cost of services like education, health care and law enforcement. But the CBO also said that costs to governments were "most likely modest."

In Oklahoma, state Rep. Dan Sullivan (R) says that a student's parents would have had to pay full taxes for years in order to cover the cost of their child's in-state tuition.

Illegal immigrants meet that standard, he said.

"Paying in-state tuition is the benefit of someone that's lived in Oklahoma and paid taxes here, so I don't think it's unfair to say you have the same access to our higher education. But you have to pay the rates that out-of-state citizens would pay," Sullivan said.

Sullivan was one of the sponsors of HB 1804, which requires students to prove their legal status in order to receive in-state tuition rates.

Oklahoma is probably the only state that has been on both sides of the debate over tuition and aid. In 2003 it passed a law making in-state tuition and state financial aid available to undocumented students.

Five years later, the state reversed course.

Like much of the country, Oklahoma has seen big growth in its Hispanic immigrant population. According to the Pew Hispanic Center, U.S. Census data showed between 1990 and 2008 the Hispanic population in Tulsa County swelled from 11,958 to 58,530. In Oklahoma County, the Hispanic population grew from 25,452 to 90,077 in 2008.

Pew estimates that 36 percent of 279,000 Hispanics in the state are foreign-born and that there between 100,000 and 200,000 illegal immigrants in the state. Still, the overall Hispanic population in Oklahoma is relatively low, just 8 percent of the state's residents.

Tim Huff, the manager for the Office of International Students and Scholars at Oklahoma State University, says the university has not really seen the full effect of HB 1804 because students who enrolled before the bill became law were permitted to continue their education at residential rates. He thinks that the university and other Oklahoma higher education institutions will really begin to see the effect of the law in the Fall of 2010 because most of the students under the old law will have graduated.

Huff does not believe undocumented students are having a negative impact on the state's higher education system. He says access to higher education is vital to the state's well-being.

"They've assimilated into our society," Huff said. "They're productive members of our society and I think we've got an obligation to try and make sure they are educated as well as they can possibly be to be productive. You don't want them to be a drag on society you want them to be productive."

Manuel, 25, is an undocumented student at Oklahoma State University. He is a junior and hopes to go to law school. Manuel has called Tulsa, Okla., his home since December of 1998, when his parents moved him, his three brothers and sister from Nuevo Leon, Mexico.

Today, Manuel and his younger brother, who is 23, find themselves in a difficult position: Although they are the youngest among their siblings, they are the only undocumented individuals in their family. Their parents and older siblings have all gained residency. However, Manuel remains optimistic about his future and feels very welcome in the Tulsa community.

"I'm hopeful that one day someone is going to look and see that I'm a good individual that... I'm a good citizen," Manuel said. "I volunteer. I serve. I help out. I have good grades. I think I'm a good person to be here and I will contribute a lot more."

Although Sullivan said he is comfortable with the current law, he understands the feeling of unfairness some undocumented students feel and he believes it is not their fault if their parents brought them into the country.

"That's been one of the biggest struggles in my mind... because you don't want to perpetuate situation where people are not educated and don't have the opportunities once they get here, but on the other hand you have to protect the taxpayer and make sure that you're not spending their money in a way that doesn't make sense," Sullivan said. "It's kind of a balancing act of how to address that."

THE HEART OF THE DEBATE — IN TEXAS

In Texas, a unique battle is brewing: A student group at Texas A&M is trying to build support to overturn the state law granted illegal immigrants the right to in-state tuition.

At least 19 student senators are supporting a resolution that would oppose the current state law. They will make a push to pass the measure during the Fall 2010 semester.

The student senators say the state law is in violation of the federal 1996 Illegal Immigration Reform and Responsibility Act because it allows colleges to provide undocumented students residential tuition rates and to deny those rates to citizens from out of state.

"That's a violation of federal law because non-residents get cheaper tuition than say someone who lives in Tennessee," said Alison Landry, one of the student senators.

Jose Luis, the student who said he was thankful to live in Texas because it allows undocumented students to receive in-state tuition, has promised to rally opposition to the student Senate resolution through the Council for Minority Student Affairs and other groups.

Ultimately, if the student Senate bill is passed, supporters plan to push state legislators to change the law.

So far Texas legislators have steadfastly supported offering in-state tuition to all Texas residents regardless of immigration status.

Because of sheer numbers, deep cultural roots and hard-fought political battles, Hispanics in Texas are a group that politicians cannot ignore.

According to the Pew Hispanic Center, Hispanics comprise 36 percent of the total population of the state — 8.8 million people. Pew estimates that Texas has between 1.3 and 1.5 million undocumented immigrants.

Though Hispanics in Texas largely vote Democratic, Republicans have made inroads. President George W. Bush, a former Texas governor and a Republican, broke ranks with his party in to support comprehensive immigration reform that would have provided a path to citizenship for undocumented immigrants already in the United States.

Current Texas Gov. Rick Perry, also a Republican, supported the law that makes undocumented students eligible for in-state tuition and state aid. Rick Noriega, a former Democratic state representative from Houston, sponsored the bill.

To Noriega the law makes good financial sense. He says creating more educated professionals will boost the state's economy.

"Now what we can do is create opportunities and access to higher education to those students who are Texans that we've already invested $100,000 each on," Noriega said. "Or ...we can look at places like Pakistan or India or China...and try to allow for additional H1 visas to allow those professionals to come to our community and take those jobs and ...that just doesn't make sense."

But Justin Pulliam, one of the student senators at Texas A&M, says the return-on-investment argument does not work because undocumented immigrants can't legally work in the United States.

"These people cannot work in America legally after they graduate," he said. "While it's a strong convincing argument that some will say, 'Well, we need to educate these people so they can get higher paying jobs in America,' that just is not the case because they legally cannot work in America."

Arizona's state treasurer, Dean Martin, echoes that argument. Martin says it makes sense for states to offer low tuition for legal residents in order to keep them in the state after college because educated workers will make more money over time, which will be a boon to the state. But he says offering that benefit to illegal immigrants will not work to a state's benefit.

"The problem is if you are here illegally, that whole incentive structure breaks down," Martin said. "Yeah, you've got a great degree, but you can't use it, legally… so there is no way you can pay the state back for its subsidy."

This is one area where Texas A&M student Jose Luis agrees with his opponents. He believes Texas's current law provides a small glimmer of hope that ends in a dead-end street.

"I see where these people come from because in a way it makes sense because Senate Bill 1528 only gives the opportunity to students to attend college but after they attend college they're not allowed to work in their profession," Jose Luis said.

THE DREAM ACT

For many undocumented students the DREAM Act (Development, Relief, and Education for Alien Minors) seems like the perfect solution.

It is a bill that has been introduced and re-introduced in Congress since 2001. Most of its supporters are Democrats. The bill would create a conditional pathway for certain undocumented students and volunteers for the military to become legalized. They would have six years of conditional legal status that would allow them to work, attend school, travel and ultimately complete the steps to gain permanent legal status.

In order to qualify for the program students would have to:
- Arrive in the country before the age of 16.
- Live in the country at least five consecutive years prior to the bill's enactment.
- Graduate from a U.S. high school or obtain a GED or get accepted to an institution of higher education.

Other requirements include a good moral character and at least a two-year commitment to higher education or military service.

According to an analysis released July 2010 by the Migration Policy Institute, the law's enactment would immediately make 726,000 unauthorized young adults eligible for conditional legal status, and of these roughly 114,000 would be eligible for permanent legal status after the six-year wait because they already have at least an associate's degree. However, during the six-year waiting period the remaining individuals would have the opportunity to complete the necessary requirements to be eligible for permanent residency. The report states that another 934,000 children under the age of 18 are potential beneficiaries.

The DREAM Act was last introduced in Congress in March 2009. The measure has garnered support from President Barack Obama as well as 40 senators co-sponsoring the bill and over 12o members of the House.

Obama also supports the measure as a part of comprehensive immigration reform.

"[W]e should stop punishing innocent young people for the actions of their parents by denying them the chance to stay here and earn an education and contribute their talents to build the country where they've grown up," Obama said in a July 2010 speech on immigration. "The DREAM Act would do this, and that's why I supported this bill as a state legislator and as a U.S. Senator—and why I continue to support it as president."

Opponents of the DREAM Act say it rewards illegal behavior and distracts from larger problems with the country's immigration system — including border security and an overly complicated procedure for immigrating legally.

Arizona State Treasurer Martin, does not support the DREAM Act, or any program that he says would provide "amnesty" for illegal immigrants. He says children are not responsible for the actions of their parents, but at age 18 they become responsible for themselves and should work on legalizing their status. Martin believes the federal bureaucracy should be reformed so people can immigrate legally, and easily.

"What, we have now is from the immigrants' point of view, is that you can either go through the bureaucracy or walk through the desert in 110 [degrees]," Martin said. "How bad is that bureaucracy when the desert looks like a good option? You've made it difficult for people to follow the law, and then you've decided, 'Well, we're not even going to enforce it.'"

Martin advocates a sponsorship program where an employer would agree to be responsible for an immigrant worker. He says students already here would have an advantage in such a program because they already know people. Martin says one of the purposes of Arizona's law is to get reform at the federal level.

"It puts pressure back on the federal government, saying, 'Look, if you will just do your job, we're glad to help those that can use the degree. But until you do your job, we're not going to subsidize a system that is really a disservice to those that are in it,'" Martin said.

Today, Lilly, the undocumented student from Arizona, works teaching English in central Phoenix where she feels privileged to help others assimilate into American society but is still waiting for the day when she can continue her college education.

"My hopes and dreams were and still are to become a neonatologist," she said. "That is a really long process; it takes about 10 years after high school and when you want to specialize it takes 16 years. So for me every minute counts. I cannot be a neonatologist when my hands are too shaky to do a procedure on a tiny little newborn."

Lilly is in the process of becoming a legal resident, but she says the it will likely take up to 10 years, which is why she is part of the Arizona DREAM Act Coalition — an alliance of students and several statewide organizations dedicated to the passage of the DREAM Act.

"I have no option as of right now. I kind of am at a standstill. I can't move forward and I definitely can't move backward," she said. "But I'm hoping and dreaming everyday and I'm advocating and fighting. I go to marches. I call senators and write letters, everything that I can do to help move the DREAM act through."

1. What are the unique concerns of immigrants trying to get into college?

2. What are some of the government programs designed to help these students, and how could they be improved?

CHAPTER 3

WHAT THE COURTS SAY

The court system has been instrumental in shaping our education system, from landmark cases like *Brown vs. Board of Education of Topeka, Kansas*, to rulings that have upheld non-discrimination. Lawsuits at the local, state, and federal levels have revolutionized access to higher education and challenged how we think of admissions to schools and how the rights enshrined in the Constitution apply to schools. Court cases are often extremely specific in their focus, but with ramifications that impact a wide-range of programs and issues. As you'll see in these court cases and debates surrounding the legal aspects of higher education, the courts are where some of our most important questions about college and who has access to education play out.

"SUIT ALLEGES RACE-BASED DISCRIMINATION IN HARVARD ADMISSIONS PRACTICES," BY THEODORE R. DELWICHE, FROM *THE HARVARD CRIMSON*, NOVEMBER 18, 2014

The legal defense group Project on Fair Representation announced a lawsuit Monday morning against Harvard University for "employing racially and ethnically discriminatory policies" in its admissions practices, according to a copy of the filed complaint published by a newly formed offshoot of the group.

"Harvard's undergraduate admissions policies and procedures have injured and continue to injure Plaintiff's members by intentionally and improperly discriminating against them on the basis of their race and ethnicity in violation of Title VI," the complaint reads. The complaint cites as the plaintiff Students for Admissions, Inc., a newly formed nonprofit law group that includes students and parents who wish to challenge the use of race in admissions practices, and calls for a permanent injunction on Harvard's policies they allege are discriminatory.

The suit comes more than six months after Edward Blum, the director of POFR, launched a site seeking students who claim they were not admitted to Harvard because of their race to participate in a potential lawsuit. Similar sites were also launched for students who were denied admission to the University of North Carolina at Chapel Hill and the University of Wisconsin-Madison. A complaint against UNC was also filed on Monday.

"It is especially disconcerting that public data shows that Harvard has purposefully limited the percentage of Asian-American freshman it admits," Blum wrote in a press release. "In fact, the number of Asian-Americans Harvard admits today is lower than it was 20-years ago, even though the number of highly qualified Asian-American applicants to Harvard has nearly doubled."

Blum could not be reached for comment on Monday afternoon.

Blum's comments mirror findings from a 2013 analysis accompanying an opinion piece published in *The New York Times* of demographic statistics for Harvard's enrollment data over nearly two decades that may indicate an Asian "quota." Dean of Admissions and Financial Aid William R. Fitzsimmons '67 said in March that Harvard does not use quotas in the admissions process.

University General Counsel Robert W. Iuliano '83 wrote in a statement that the University's admissions policies are "fully compliant" with the law.

"In his seminal opinion in *Regents of University of California v. Bakke*, Justice Powell specially cited to the Harvard College admissions plan in describing a legally sound approach to admissions," Iuliano wrote Monday afternoon. "Then and now, the College considers each applicant through an individualized, holistic review having the goal of creating a vibrant academic community that exposes students to a wide-range of differences: background, ideas, experiences, talents and aspirations. The University's admissions processes remain fully compliant with all legal requirements and are essential to the pedagogical objectives that underlie Harvard's educational mission."

The 120-page complaint against Harvard claims that the University uses "racial balancing" in its admissions decisions, even when allegedly "race-neutral alternatives can achieve diversity." The complaint also detailed a long history of Harvard's admissions policies, including the widely discussed discrimination of Jewish applicants in the early 20th century and the pushing for a holistic admissions process.

In the past, Blum has helped fund high-profile cases, including the 2013 *Fisher vs. University of Texas*, challenging affirmative action policies at school. Whereas Abigail Fisher was a white female, the complaint filed Monday focuses on discrimination against Asian-American students.

Students for Fair Admissions has a least one member who was denied admissions to the Harvard College Class of 2018, according to the complaint. That individual is allegedly an Asian-American first generation student who graduated top from his or her high school and achieved score of 36 on the ACT, while participating in several other extracurricular activities.

That same applicant enrolled at a top 20 school, as outlined by U.S. News and World report, that does not preference race or ethnicity in admissions decisions and "intends to seek transfer to Harvard when it ceases the use of race or ethnicity as admissions preference."

1. What is racial balancing? Why might this be considered discriminatory?

2. Blum previously funded a lawsuit by a white woman named Abigail Fisher against the University of Texas, charging discrimination on her race. How might this fact influence how you view this new lawsuit?

EXCERPT FROM *CANNON V. UNIVERSITY OF CHICAGO 441 U.S. 677(1979)*, FROM THE SUPREME COURT OF THE UNITED STATES, MAY 14, 1979

MR. JUSTICE STEVENS delivered the opinion of the Court.

Petitioner's complaints allege that her applications for admission to medical school were denied by the respondents because she is a woman.[1] Accepting the truth of those allegations for the purpose of its decision, the Court of Appeals held that petitioner has no right of action against respondents that may be asserted in a federal court. 559 F. 2d 1063. We granted certiorari to review that holding. 438 U. S. 914.

Only two facts alleged in the complaints are relevant to our decision. First, petitioner was excluded from participation in the respondents' medical education programs because of her sex. Second, these education programs were receiving federal financial assistance at the time of her exclusion. These facts, admitted arguendo by respondents' motion to dismiss the complaints, establish a violation of § 901 (a) of Title IX of the Education Amendments of 1972 (hereinafter Title IX).[2]

That section, in relevant part, provides:

"No person in the United States shall, on the basis of sex, be excluded from participation in, be denied the benefits of, or be subjected to discrimination under any education program or activity receiving Federal financial assistance ... "[3]

The statute does not, however, expressly authorize a private right of action by a person injured by a violation of § 901. For that reason, and because it concluded that no private remedy should be inferred, the District Court granted the respondents' motions to dismiss. 406 F. Supp. 1257, 1259.

The Court of Appeals agreed that the statute did not contain an implied private remedy. Noting that § 902 of Title IX establishes a procedure for the termination of federal financial support for institutions violating § 901, the Court of Appeals concluded that Congress intended that remedy to be the exclusive means of enforcement. [4] It recognized that the statute was patterned after Title VI of the Civil Rights Act of 1964 (hereinafter Title VI), [5] but rejected petitioner's argument that Title VI included an implied private cause of action. 559 F. 2d, at 1071-1075.

After the Court of Appeal's decision was announced, Congress enacted the Civil Rights Attorney's Fees Awards Act of 1976, 90 Stat. 2641, which authorizes an award of fees to prevailing private parties in actions to enforce Title IX.[6] The court therefore granted a petition for rehearing to consider whether, in the light of that statute, its original interpretation of Title IX had been correct. After receiving additional briefs, the court concluded that the 1976 Act was not intended to create a remedy that did not previously exist.[7] The court also noted that the Department of Health, Education, and Welfare had taken the position that a private cause of action under Title IX should be implied,[8] but the court disagreed with that agency's interpretation of the Act. In sum, it adhered to its original view, 559 F. 2d, at 1077-1080.

The Court of Appeals quite properly devoted careful attention to this question of statutory construction. As our recent cases—particularly *Cort v. Ash*, 422

U. S. 66—demonstrate, the fact that a federal statute has been violated and some person harmed does not automatically give rise to a private cause of action in favor of that person. Instead, before concluding that Congress intended to make a remedy available to a special class of litigants, a court must carefully analyze the four factors that Cort identifies as indicative of such an intent.[9] Our review of those factors persuades us, however, that the Court of Appeals reached the wrong conclusion and that petitioner does have a statutory right to pursue her claim that respondents rejected her application on the basis of her sex. After commenting on each of the four factors, we shall explain why they are not overcome by respondents' countervailing arguments.

I

First, the threshold question under Cort is whether the statute was enacted for the benefit of a special class of which the plaintiff is a member. That question is answered by looking to the language of the statute itself. Thus, the statutory reference to "any employee of any such common carrier" in the 1893 legislation requiring railroads to equip their cars with secure "grab irons or handholds," see 27 Stat. 532, 531, made "irresistible" the Court's earliest "inference of a private right of action"—in that case in favor of a railway employee who was injured when a grab iron gave way. *Texas & Pacific R. Co. v. Rigsby*, 241 U. S. 33, 40.[10]

Similarly, it was statutory language describing the special class to be benefited by § 5 of the Voting Rights Act of 1965[11] that persuaded the Court that private parties within that class were implicitly authorized to seek a declaratory judgment against a covered State. *Allen v. State Board of Elections*, 393 U. S. 544, 554-555.[12] The dispositive language in that statute—"no person shall be denied the right to vote for failure to comply with [a new state enactment covered by, but not approved under, § 5]"—is remarkably similar to the language used by Congress in Title IX. See n. 3, supra.

The language in these statutes—which expressly identifies the class Congress intended to benefit—contrasts sharply with statutory language customarily found in criminal statutes, such as that construed in Cort, supra, and other laws enacted for the protection of the general public.[13] There would be far less reason to infer a private remedy in favor of individual persons if Congress, instead of drafting Title IX with an unmistakable focus on the benefited class, had written it simply as a ban on discriminatory conduct by recipients of federal funds or as a prohibition against the disbursement of public funds to educational institutions engaged in discriminatory practices.[14]

Unquestionably, therefore, the first of the four factors identified in Cort favors the implication of a private cause of action. Title IX explicitly confers a benefit on persons discriminated against on the basis of sex, and petitioner is clearly a member of that class for whose special benefit the statute was enacted.

Second, the Cort analysis requires consideration of legislative history. We must recognize, however, that the legislative history of a statute that does not expressly create or deny a private remedy will typically be equally silent or ambiguous on the question. Therefore, in situations such as the present one "in which it is clear that federal law has granted a class of persons certain rights, it is not necessary to show an intention to create a private cause of action, although an explicit purpose to deny such cause of action would be controlling." Cort, 422 U. S., at 82 (emphasis in original).[15] But this is not the typical case. Far from evidencing any purpose to deny a private cause of action, the history of Title IX rather plainly indicates that Congress intended to create such a remedy.

Title IX was patterned after Title VI of the Civil Rights Act of 1964.[16] Except for the substitution of the word "sex" in Title IX to replace the words "race, color, or national origin" in Title VI, the two statutes use identical language to describe the benefited class.[17] Both statutes provide the same administrative mechanism for terminating federal financial support for institutions engaged in prohibited discrimination.[18] Neither statute expressly mentions a private remedy for the person excluded from participation in a federally funded program. The drafters of Title IX explicitly assumed that it would be interpreted and applied as Title VI had been during the preceding eight years.[19]

In 1972 when Title IX was enacted, the critical language in Title VI had already been construed as creating a private remedy. Most particularly, in 1967, a distinguished panel of the Court of Appeals for the Fifth Circuit squarely decided this issue in an opinion that was repeatedly cited with approval and never questioned during the ensuing five years.[20] In addition, at least a dozen other federal courts reached similar conclusions in the same or related contexts during those years.[21] It is always appropriate to assume that our elected representatives, like other citizens, know the law; in this case, because of their repeated references to Title VI and its modes of enforcement, we are especially justified in presuming both that those representatives were aware of the prior interpretation of Title VI and that that interpretation reflects their intent with respect to Title IX.

Moreover, in 1969, in *Allen v. State Board of Elections*, 393 U. S. 544, this court had interpreted the comparable language in § 5 of the Voting Rights Act as sufficient to authorize a private remedy.[22] Indeed, during the period between the enactment of Title VI in 1964 and the enactment of Title IX in 1972, this Court had consistently found implied remedies— often in cases much less clear than this.[23] It was after 1972 that this Court decided *Cort v. Ash* and the other cases cited by the Court of Appeals in support of its strict construction of the remedial aspect of the statute.[24] We, of course, adhere to the strict approach followed in our recent cases, but our evaluation of congressional action in 1972 must take into account its contemporary legal context. In sum, it is not only appropriate but also realistic to presume that Congress was thoroughly familiar with these unusually important precedents from this and other federal courts and that it expected its enactment to be interpreted in conformity with them.

It is not, however, necessary to rely on these presumptions. The package of statutes of which Title IX is one part also contains a provision whose language and history demonstrate that Congress itself understood Title VI, and thus its companion, Title IX, as creating a private remedy. Section 718 of the Education Amendments authorizes federal courts to award attorney's fees to the prevailing parties, other than the United States, in private actions brought against public educational agencies to enforce Title VI in the context of elementary and secondary education.[25] The language of this provision explicitly presumes the availability of private suits to enforce Title VI in the education context.[26] For many such suits, no express cause of action was then available; hence Congress must have assumed that one could be implied under Title VI itself.[27] That assumption was made explicit during the debates on § 718.[28] It was also aired during the debates on other provisions in the Education Amendments of 1972[29] and on Title IX itself,[30] and is consistent with the Executive Branch's apparent understanding of Title VI at the time.[31]

Finally, the very persistence—before 1972 and since, among judges and executive officials, as well as among litigants and their counsel,[32] and even implicit in decisions of this Court[33]— of the assumption that both Title VI and Title IX created a private right of action for the victims of illegal discrimination and the absence of legislative action to change that assumption provide further evidence that Congress at least acquiesces in, and apparently affirms, that assumption. See n. 7, supra. We have no doubt that Congress intended to create Title IX remedies comparable to those available under Title VI and that it understood Title VI as authorizing an implied private cause of action for victims of the prohibited discrimination.[34]

Third, under Cort, a private remedy should not be implied if it would frustrate the underlying purpose of the legislative scheme. On the other hand, when that remedy is necessary or at least helpful to the accomplishment of the statutory purpose, the Court is decidedly receptive to its implication under the statute.[35]

Title IX, like its model Title VI, sought to accomplish two related, but nevertheless somewhat different, objectives. First, Congress wanted to avoid the use of federal resources to support discriminatory practices; second, it wanted to provide individual citizens effective protection against those practices. Both of these purposes were repeatedly identified in the debates on the two statutes.[36]

The first purpose is generally served by the statutory procedure for the termination of federal financial support for institutions engaged in discriminatory practices.[37] That remedy is, however, severe and often may not provide an appropriate means of accomplishing the second purpose if merely an isolated violation has occurred.[38] In that situation, the violation might be remedied more efficiently by an order requiring an institution to accept an applicant who had been improperly excluded.[39] Moreover, in that kind of situation it makes little sense to impose on an individual, whose only interest is in obtaining a benefit for herself, or on HEW, the burden of demonstrating that an institution's practices are so pervasively discriminatory that a complete cutoff of federal funding is appropriate. The award of individual relief to a private litigant who has prosecuted her own suit is not only sensible but is also fully consistent with—and in some cases even necessary to—the orderly enforcement of the statute.[40]

The Department of Health, Education, and Welfare, which is charged with the responsibility for administering Title IX, perceives no inconsistency between the private remedy and the public remedy.[41] On the contrary, the agency takes the unequivocal position that the individual remedy will provide effective assistance to achieving the statutory purposes. See n. 8, supra. The agency's position is unquestionably correct.[42]

Fourth, the final inquiry suggested by Cort is whether implying a federal remedy is inappropriate because the subject matter involves an area basically of concern to the States. No such problem is raised by a prohibition against invidious discrimination of any sort, including that on the basis of sex. Since the Civil War, the Federal Government and the federal courts have been the " `primary and powerful reliances' " in protecting citizens against such discrimination. *Steffel v. Thompson*, 415 U. S. 452, 464 (emphasis in original), quoting F. Frankfurter & J. Landis, The Business of the Supreme Court 65 (1928). Moreover, it is the expenditure of federal funds that provides the justification for this particular statutory prohibition. There can be no question but that this aspect of the Cort analysis supports the implication of a private federal remedy.

In sum, there is no need in this case to weigh the four Cort factors; all of them support the same result. Not only the words and history of Title IX, but also its subject matter and underlying purposes, counsel implication of a cause of action in favor of private victims of discrimination.

1. What was the purpose of Title IX, according to this court ruling?

2. What role does gender discrimination play in admissions, and what can be done to counter it?

"EXPLAINER: CRUCIAL TEXAS CASE ON RACE CONSIDERATIONS IN COLLEGE ADMISSIONS," BY LILIANA M. GARCES AND GARY ORTFIELD WITH THE PARTNERSHIP OF PENNSYLVANIA STATE UNIVERSITY AND THE UNIVERSITY OF CALIFORNIA, FROM *THE CONVERSATION*, JULY 2, 2015

Twelve years ago, after an epic legal battle over the University of Michigan's affirmative action admissions policy in its law school and undergraduate school, the Supreme Court upheld the importance of student body diversity for the institution's educational mission and the need to consider race as a factor in admissions.

The case, *Grutter v Bollinger* (2003), which also relied on a prior case that dated back to 1978, *University of California v Bakke*, cited extensive evidence about the importance of a racially and ethnically diverse student body.

However, in 2012 the Supreme Court reopened the issue, with the *Fisher v University of Texas* case.

Abigail Fisher is a white female applicant who applied to the university in 2008 and was denied admission. She then sued the University of Texas at Austin on the grounds that the university's race-conscious admissions policy violated the equal protection clause of the Fourteenth Amendment.

Now the case is, once again, back before the Supreme Court (after having been decided, again, in UT-Austin's favor by a lower court and appealed, again, by Fisher) and will be heard in the 2015-2016 term.

While the case raises questions specific to UT-Austin's program, it is also possible that the Supreme Court may further limit the use of race in higher education admissions policies for institutions across the nation.

This could be a historic decision, following a term in which the court decided to severely curtail the Voting Rights Act and uphold the constitutionality of a ban on affirmative action in Michigan.

FISHER: ROUND 1

The Fisher case was expected to be a fundamental decision on affirmative action in universities.

When the court first agreed to hear the case in 2012, the social science community came together, along with the Civil Rights Project at UCLA, to support the race-conscious admissions policy at UT-Austin.

The American Educational Research Association, along with numerous other scholarly organizations, filed a brief summarizing the extensive research demonstrating the educational benefits of a racially diverse student body.

Some 444 social scientists from 172 institutions across the nation submitted a brief for which the lead author of this article served as counsel of record, outlining the evidence demonstrating the limits of so-called race-neutral policies in achieving racial diversity.

In its decision in 2013, the court reaffirmed the important value of educational diversity.

However, a contentious issue was left unresolved: the court did not reach a judgment on the key question of whether there was a nonracial way to achieve the diversity that would make consideration of race unnecessary and therefore illegal under the court's standards.

CAN DIVERSITY BE ACHIEVED BY IGNORING RACE?

The decision was subsequently described as a "compromise" in which seven of the eight justices who heard the case agreed to send it back to the lower court for review.

Only Justice Ruth Bader Ginsburg dissented, on the grounds that she would have found the policy constitutional without further review by the lower court.

The decision clarified that the means institutions use to further their interest in diversity required judicial overview, meaning that a judge may not rely on the judgment of the university alone, or defer to its determination, but will require evidence that supports the institution's decisions.

In doing so, the decision also clarified the importance of considering workable race-neutral alternatives.

If a nonracial approach could promote diversity "about as well and at tolerable administrative expense," then the university could not consider race directly. This placed a high, but not insurmountable, bar to justify ongoing consideration of race in admissions policies.

The justices asked the lower court, which had appeared to defer to the university's judgment on the necessity of considering race, to reach its own decision on this issue.

The case went to the Fifth Circuit, which reheard the case and decided, for the second time, that UT-Austin's admissions policy met the requirements of the court's clarified standard in Fisher and that of past cases.

Fisher, however, appealed arguing that the Fifth Circuit still had not applied the test correctly.

FISHER: ROUND 2

In the first round, the lawyers for Abigail Fisher said they were not asking the court to reverse prior cases. What they argued, instead, was that UT Austin's race-conscious policy was not necessary because other laws in the state, such as the Top Ten Percent Plan, allowed the university to achieve what the Fisher lawyers saw as sufficient racial diversity.

This seems to be the same argument they are presenting in this second round (though that could change as the briefing develops).

Under the plan, students who graduate at the top 10% of their class can be automatically admitted to any campus of the university they wish to attend. The university was able to achieve some level of racial diversity with the plan.

But UT-Austin found that as an alternative to the direct consideration of race in admissions, it was insufficient. The university thus sought to complement the 10% plan with a race-conscious review process.

After the remand in 2013, the Fifth Circuit agreed, but one judge strongly dissented, arguing that the university had failed to provide evidence showing that the 10% plan had not produced sufficient diversity.

This judge also argued that the court had not been sufficiently demanding in examining the university's justifications: the university's goals, he said, were vague and the "critical mass" of diversity the university needed not well-defined.

NEED TO CONSIDER RACE

The concept of critical mass has been at the center of affirmative action litigation efforts since *Grutter*, and will be central again in this second round in *Fisher*.

Universities seek to attain it because token representation of a minority group produces problems of extreme isolation and gives little opportunity for other students to interact with minority students.

Opponents challenge it as a goal that is ill-defined and ask for a definition that specifies a number (even though such a number could be considered an illegal quota under the court's decision in *Bakke*).

My own analysis shows that the notion of critical mass cannot be reduced to a number, as it depends on a number of contextual factors necessary to obtain the benefits of diversity.

Other research also shows that when race is not considered in a holistic admissions process, as has been the case at institutions in the eight states that ban affirmative action policies, racial and ethnic diversity in the student body declines significantly, especially in highly selective campuses.

These declines have taken place at colleges and universities, in graduate education and across different fields of study, including engineering, natural sciences, social sciences and humanities, and in the important field of medicine.

NEED FOR DIVERSITY

In recent years, even with affirmative action in the great majority of states, students of color and low-income students are earning college degrees at lower rates than their peers, deepening the concern of civil rights groups about the Court's new move.

The court's decision to hear the case again was also immediately criticized by the Leadership Conference on Civil Rights, representing more than 200 civil rights groups.

As with the first round, one of the justices who had recused herself earlier – Justice Kagan – will not participate, given her prior role as solicitor general when the case was being litigated earlier. With one fewer vote than usual, there is a possibility for a tie, which could leave the lower court decision supporting the University of Texas in place.

The court is likely to hear from many research and higher education organizations who can present evidence via friend-of-the-court briefs.

In the weeks before briefs are to be submitted to the court, researchers working in this field will be discussing the issues, updating research syntheses, and, once again, seeking to offer critical data to aid the court's deliberations and to inform the broader public not yet aware of the potential consequences of the coming decision.

Our nation's colleges play a critical role in preparing students for a multiracial society. It is our hope that the court will be guided by the weight of the social science research documenting the myriad educational benefits of diversity and the need to consider race, in a limited fashion, to meet their educational mission.

1. How has the Supreme Court shaped college admissions?

2. Are college and university admissions biased, according to this article? Why or why not?

"WHAT ABIGAIL FISHER'S AFFIRMATIVE ACTION CASE WAS REALLY ABOUT," BY NIKOLE HANNAH-JONES, FROM *PROPUBLICA*, JUNE 23 2016

The Supreme Court has upheld the University of Texas's consideration of race in admissions. The case had been brought by Abigail Fisher, who argued she had been denied admission because of her race.

In 2013, ProPublica's Nikole Hannah-Jones highlighted an overlooked, deeply ironic fact about the case: When one looked at Fisher's arguments, she had not actually been denied admission because she is white, but rather because of her inadequate academic achievements. Read that analysis, originally published March 18, 2013, below.

When the NAACP began challenging Jim Crow laws across the South, it knew that, in the battle for public opinion, the particular plaintiffs mattered as much as the facts of the case. The group meticulously selected the people who would elicit both sympathy and outrage, who were pristine in form and character. And they had to be ready to step forward at the exact moment when both public sentiment and the legal system might be swayed.

That's how Oliver Brown, a hard-working welder and assistant pastor in Topeka, Kan., became the lead plaintiff in the lawsuit that would obliterate the separate but equal doctrine. His daughter, whose third-grade innocence posed a searing rebuff to legal segregation, became its face.

Nearly 60 years after that Supreme Court victory, which changed the nation, conservatives freely admit they have stolen that page from the NAACP's legal playbook as they attempt to roll back many of the civil rights group's landmark triumphs.

In 23-year-old Abigail Noel Fisher they've put forward their version of the perfect plaintiff to challenge the use of race in college admissions decisions.

Publicly, Fisher and her supporters, chief among them the conservative activist who conceived of the case, have worked to make Fisher the symbol of racial victimization in modern America. As their narratives goes, she did everything right. She worked hard, received good grades, and rounded out her high school years with an array of extracurricular activities. But she was cheated, they say, her dream snatched away by a university that closed its doors to her because she had been born the wrong color: White.

The daughter of suburban Sugar Land, Texas, played the cello. Since the second grade, she said, she dreamed of carrying on the family tradition by joining her sister and father among the ranks of University of Texas at Austin alumni.

And the moment for her to lend her name to the lawsuit might never be riper: The Supreme Court has seated its most conservative bench since the 1930s. The Court is expected to issue a decision any week now in what is considered one of the most important civil rights cases in years.

On a YouTube video posted by Edward Blum, a 1973 University of Texas graduate whose nonprofit organization is bankrolling the lawsuit, she is soft-spoken, her strawberry blond hair tucked behind one ear. Not even a swipe of lip gloss adorns her girlish face.

"There were people in my class with lower grades who weren't in all the activities I was in, who were being accepted into UT, and the only other difference between us was the color of our skin," she says. "I was taught from the time I was a little girl that any kind of discrimination was wrong. And for an institution of higher learning to act this way makes no sense to me. What kind of example does it set for others?"

It's a deeply emotional argument delivered by an earnest young woman, one that's been quoted over and over again.

Except there's a problem. The claim that race cost Fisher her spot at the University of Texas isn't really true.

In the hundreds of pages of legal filings, Fisher's lawyers spend almost no time arguing that Fisher would have gotten into the university but for her race.

If you're confused, it is no doubt in part because of how Blum, Fisher and others have shaped the dialogue as the case worked its way to the country's top court.

Journalists and bloggers have written dozens of articles on the case, including profiles of Fisher and Blum. News networks have aired panel after panel about the future of affirmative action. Yet for all the front-page attention, angry debate and exchanges before the justices, some of the more fundamental elements of the case have been little reported.

Race probably had nothing to do with the University of Texas's decision to deny admission to Abigail Fisher.

In 2008, the year Fisher sent in her application, competition to get into the crown jewel of the Texas university system was stiff. Students entering through the university's Top 10 program — a mechanism that granted automatic admission to any teen who graduated in the upper 10 percent of his or her high school class — claimed 92 percent of the in-state spots.

Fisher said in news reports that she hoped for the day universities selected students "solely based on their merit and if they work hard for it." But Fisher failed to graduate in the top 10 percent of her class, meaning she had to compete for the limited number of spaces up for grabs.

She and other applicants who did not make the cut were evaluated based on two scores. One allotted points for grades and test scores. The other, called a personal achievement index, awarded points for two required essays, leadership, activities, service and "special circumstances." Those included socioeconomic status of the student or the student's school, coming from a home with a single parent or one where English wasn't spoken. And race.

Those two scores, combined, determine admission.

Even among those students, Fisher did not particularly stand out. Court records show her grade point average (3.59) and SAT scores (1180 out of 1600) were good but not great for the highly selective flagship university. The school's rejection rate that year for the remaining 841 openings was higher than the turn-down rate for students trying to get into Harvard.

As a result, university officials claim in court filings that even if Fisher received points for her race and every other personal achievement factor, the letter she received in the mail still would have said no.

It's true that the university, for whatever reason, offered provisional admission to some students with lower test scores and grades than Fisher. Five of those students were black or Latino. Forty-two were white.

Neither Fisher nor Blum mentioned those 42 applicants in interviews. Nor did they acknowledge the 168 black and Latino students with grades as good as or better than Fisher's who were also denied entry into the university that year. Also left unsaid is the fact that Fisher turned down a standard UT offer under which she could have gone to the university her sophomore year if she earned a 3.2 GPA at another Texas university school in her freshman year.

In an interview last month, Blum agreed Fisher's credentials and circumstances make it difficult to argue — as he and his supporters have so ardently in public — that but for her race Fisher would have been a Longhorn.

"There are some Anglo students who had lower grades than Abby who were admitted also," Blum told ProPublica. "Litigation like this is not a black and white paradigm."

Blum started his one-man nonprofit, the Project on Fair Representation, in 2005. The organization is funded by deep-pocketed conservatives to, according to its website, influence "jurisprudence, public policy, and public attitudes regarding race and ethnicity" in voting, education, contracting and employment. To do so, Blum — who is not a lawyer — helps arrange pro bono representation to fight race-based policies that were meant to address inequalities.

According to a Reuters profile, Blum has brought at least a dozen lawsuits against such programs and laws — including four that made it to the Supreme Court. He has two on the current docket, Fisher and the Shelby County, Ala., case challenging a key provision of the Voting Rights Act.

In the Fisher case, while the young woman may have lent her name to the lawsuit, the case before the Court has very little to do with her. Her name appears just five times in the thousands of words that make up the body of the complaint. She has already gone on to graduate from Louisiana State University, her second choice, and is working in finance at a firm in Austin.

Asked by a news reporter what harm she had suffered, she cited only her inability to tap into UT's alumni network and possibly missing out on a better first job. If she wins, Fisher seeks only the return of her application fee and housing deposit — a grand total of $100 in damages.

So while the Fisher case has been billed as a referendum on affirmative action, its backers have significantly grander ambitions: They seek to make the case a referendum on the 14th Amendment itself. At issue is whether the Constitution's equal protection clause, drafted by Congress during Reconstruction to ensure the rights of black Americans, also prohibits the use of race to help them overcome the nation's legacy of racism.

The Supreme Court has never ruled that the Constitution bars any and all laws and government programs that consider race. But Blum and his supporters, seeing an opening with the current Court, seek to overturn more than a century of precedent.

The true crux of the suit is not Fisher's failed application, but that government officials violate the constitutional rights of white Americans when they consider race in a way that might help African-Americans and Latinos.

"An argument can be made that it is simply impossible to tease out down to the last student who would have been admitted, and who would have not been admitted, had they been a different skin color," Blum said. "What we know is skin color is weighed and ethnicity is weighed by the University of Texas in their admissions process, and that alone is enough to strike down the plan."

Blum and his supporters say the reasoning is simple. The Constitution is colorblind and the equal protection clause of the 14th Amendment prohibits the government from treating people differently because of race.

It's an argument first successfully championed by the NAACP and other civil rights groups, most notably in the landmark *Brown v. Board of Education* case, in which the Supreme Court declared the notion of "separate but equal" to be a fallacy.

"In its history, colorblindness has this progressive, anti-racist push behind it," said Ian Haney-López, a constitutional scholar at the University of California, Berkeley School of Law.

But following the Brown decision, the very groups that had ardently — and violently — defended laws mandating separation by race used the notion of a colorblind Constitution to challenge court orders to integrate schools.

"They began to say, yes, the Constitution is colorblind, and so the state cannot distinguish between races when it tried to remedy segregation," he said.

As a result of Southern resistance, it would take six years after Brown before 6-year old Ruby Bridges, wearing crisp white socks and black-bowed shoes, became the first black student to attend a white elementary school in the South. The image of the diminutive brown-skinned girl who needed U.S. marshals to protect her from an angry white mob inspired Norman Rockwell to preserve the moment in a painting that now hangs in the White House occupied by the first black president.

Initially, the Supreme Court unambiguously knocked those arguments down. In a 1971 ruling, it said that government could not mandate colorblindness when doing so would defeat the integration requirement of *Brown v. Board of Education.* A few years later, in a ruling on affirmative action, Justice Harry Blackmun wrote, "In order to get beyond racism, we must first take race into account. There is no other way."

But as the Supreme Court's make-up has grown more conservative, it has taken up a steady stream of so-called reverse discrimination cases, in which white plaintiffs have argued that race-specific measures born of the civil rights movement discriminate against white Americans and violate the 14th Amendment.

Supreme Court decisions have eroded programs and laws that use race to remedy inequalities, but not eliminated them altogether. And in a 2003 opinion written by centrist Sandra Day O'Connor, the justices narrowly upheld affirmative action in college admissions when it is the only means to ensure diversity.

But the Court's make-up changed in what scholars consider a significant way when Samuel Alito, considered the third most conservative Supreme Court justice since 1937, replaced O'Connor in 2006. Since then, several justices have made their constitutional disdain for race-conscious programs known. In a controversial

2007 decision, Chief Justice John Roberts sent a clear message when he used the equal protection argument at play in *Brown v. Board of Education* to strike down voluntary desegregation plans in schools.

Evoking a colorblind Constitution, Roberts said, "The way to stop discriminating on the basis of race, is to stop discriminating on the basis of race."

And just last month during oral arguments over the constitutionality of a key aspect of the Voting Rights Act, Justice Antonin Scalia derisively called what's considered the most successful civil rights law in history a "racial entitlement."

Public opinion on race has changed over time as well. In the 1950s, surveys show, most white Americans believed that black Americans faced substantial discrimination but that they themselves experienced little. Today, despite gaping disparities between black and white Americans in income, education, health care, homeownership, employment and college admissions, a majority of white Americans now believe they are just as likely, or more likely, to face discrimination as black Americans.

Blum chose the University of Texas to mount what could be a decisive challenge to affirmative action in college admissions because it already had what was regarded as a "race-neutral" process — the Top 10 program. Since many Texas high schools remain segregated, taking the top 10 percent of students from black and Latino high schools ensured a substantial population of students of color at the UT.

As a consequence, Blum believed he could challenge whether the additional use of race to fill out the entering class passed constitutional muster.

To get standing in court, Blum needed a victim. That's when he started looking for a version of the Brown family, someone who could represent the arguable hurt caused when public officials used race.

This approach, too, mirrors an NAACP tactic from half a century ago. Then, knowing the Supreme Court was unlikely to throw out segregation in one fell swoop, the civil rights group brought a narrower challenge to segregated school facilities first.

One of those cases, ironically, targeted the same university as Blum — the University of Texas at Austin. The university, which had been closed to black students since its founding, denied the law school application of Heman Marion Sweatt because the state constitution required that black and white students attend separate schools.

Because Texas had no black law school, the NAACP sued, arguing that the state violated the constitutional mandate to provide equal facilities for black and white students. The Supreme Court ruled that the hastily put together black law school created to avoid admitting Sweatt could not possibly be equal. It ordered Texas to admit Sweatt as its first black student in 1950.

That suit launched the stone that would shatter separate but equal just four years later when the Court struck down segregation in schools in *Brown*.

Blum and his supporters hope to use the Fisher case, and the 14th Amendment challenge to the Voting Rights Act that Blum is also behind, in the same way.

According to Blum, the Constitution sees affirmative action policies — in college, in contracting, in employment — and Jim Crow laws as twin evils.

"I don't see the distinction," he said.

But several constitutional scholars interviewed for this piece dispute this notion. Neil Siegel of Duke University called this interpretation of the 14th Amendment "perverse." Georgetown law professor Girardeau A. Spann called it "discriminatory."

While the 14th Amendment doesn't mention race, the drafters went on to pass race-specific legislation aimed at helping former slaves and other black Americans overcome more than a century of racial oppression.

Erwin Chemerinsky, founding dean of the University of California, Irvine School of Law, said that the concept of colorblindness holds great rhetorical appeal but that "there is no basis for concluding that the 14th Amendment equal protection clause requires colorblindness." In drafting the 14th Amendment, he said, Congress recognized "an enormous difference between a white majority disadvantaging minorities and a white majority acting to remedy past discrimination."

Conservatives challenging these types of programs purport to champion the legacy of the civil rights movement, Haney-Lopez said, but the historical roots of their efforts are much more cynical.

"I think that is incredibly important that people realize that today's proponents of colorblindness pretend that they are the heirs to Thurgood Marshall and John Marshall Harlan," he said. "But that is a lie. They are the heirs of Southern resistance to integration. And the colorblindness arguments that they use come directly from the Southern efforts to defeat *Brown v. Board of Education*."

Ilya Shapiro, a senior constitutional studies fellow at the Cato Institute, which filed an amicus brief supporting Fisher, thinks otherwise.

"I am not going to speak to anyone else's motives. It is unfair to paint people with the Jim Crow brush because they have those kinds of arguments," he said. "I don't like people being judged based on the color of their skin." If a program "treats people different because one has a different skin color, I find that offensive and I think the Constitution does as well."

But when asked why the drafters created programs targeted to black Americans if they did not intend the Constitution to allow the government to use race to help minority groups, Shapiro said, "It was a curious period."

At the same time Congress drafted the equal protection clause, he said, it also "voted for segregated schools in the District of Columbia."

That example is the very same one that segregationists Strom Thurmond and Richard Brevard Russell used when they drafted the 1956 Southern Manifesto urging officials to resist the Supreme Court's use of the equal protection clause to overturn school segregation.

The impact of a ruling that bans all racial considerations by universities, employers and governments "could have devastating impact on the ability to overcome past inequalities," Siegel said.

Few experts think Blum and his supporters are apt to win that big a victory in the Fisher case. And so he will likely be on the hunt again for another case, and another perfect plaintiff.

1. What role has race played in education? What role might it play now?

2. According to this article, are affirmative action programs still important? Why or why not?

EXCERPT FROM *MISSISSIPPI UNIVERSITY FOR WOMEN V. HOGAN, 458 U.S. 718 (1982)*, FROM THE UNITED STATES SUPREME COURT, JULY 1, 1982

Held: The policy of petitioner Mississippi University for Women (MUW), a state-supported university which has from its inception limited its enrollment to women, of denying otherwise qualified males (such as respondent) the right to enroll for credit in its School of Nursing violates the Equal Protection Clause of the Fourteenth Amendment. Pp. 458 U. S. 723-733.

(a) The party seeking to uphold a statute that classifies individuals on the basis of their gender must carry the burden of showing an "exceedingly persuasive justification" for the classification. *Kirchberg v. Feenstra*, 450 U. S. 455, 450 U. S. 461; *Personnel Administrator of Mass. v. Feeney*, 442 U. S. 256, 442 U. S. 273. The burden is met only by showing at least that the classification serves "important governmental objectives and that the discriminatory means employed" are "substantially related to the achievement of those objectives." *Wengler v. Druggists Mutual Insurance Co.*, 446 U. S. 142, 446 U. S. 150. The test must be applied free of fixed notions concerning the roles and abilities of males and females. Pp. 458 U. S. 723-727.

(b) The single-sex admissions policy of MUW's School of Nursing cannot be justified on the asserted ground that it compensates for discrimination against women and, therefore, constitutes educational affirmative action. A State can evoke a compensatory purpose to justify an otherwise discriminatory classification only if members of the gender benefited by the classification actually suffer a disadvantage related to the classification. Rather than compensating for discriminatory barriers faced by women, MUW's policy tends to perpetuate the stereotyped view of nursing as an exclusively woman's job. Moreover, the State has not shown that the gender-based classification is substantially and directly related to its proposed compensatory objective. To the contrary, MUW's policy of permitting men to attend classes as auditors fatally undermines its claim that women, at least those in the School of Nursing, are adversely affected by the presence of men. Thus, the State has fallen far short of establishing the "exceedingly persuasive justification" needed to sustain the gender-based classification. Pp.458 U. S. 727-731.

(c) Nor can the exclusion of men from MUW's School of Nursing be justified on the basis of the language of § 901(a)(5) of Title IX of the Education Amendments of 1972, which exempts from § 901(a)'s general prohibition of gender discrimination in federally funded education programs the admissions policies of public institutions of undergraduate higher education "that traditionally and continually from [their] establishment [have] had a policy of admitting only students of one sex." It is not clear that, as argued by the State, Congress enacted the statute pursuant to its power granted by § 5 of the

Fourteenth Amendment to enforce that Amendment, and thus placed a limitation upon the broad prohibitions of the Equal Protection Clause. Rather, Congress apparently intended, at most, to create an exemption from Title IX's requirements. In any event, Congress' power under § 5 "is limited to adopting measures to enforce the guarantees of the Amendment; § 5 grants Congress no power to restrict, abrogate, or dilute these guarantees."

1. According to the court, is it discrimination for single-sex schools to deny admission to the opposite sex?

2. In what cases are single-sex admissions allowed, according to this decision? Why might schools have single-sex admissions policies, and why might they not?

CHAPTER 4

WHAT ADVOCATES AND ADVOCACY GROUPS SAY

E ducation is a topic many people from a diverse range of backgrounds are very passionate about, and as a result there are many advocates fighting for its future. But advocacy groups do more than lobby for policy changes. Advocacy groups and nonprofits are at the forefront of understanding how education works in this country, where there is opportunity for growth, and how students are being impacted by policy. While most focus on specific populations, such as students with disabilities or immigrants, their findings can highlight issues in college admissions that face all students and impact higher education as a whole. The articles in this chapter examine important issues in college admissions that advocates have fought and continue to fight for.

"LEARNING DISABILITIES AND THE LAW: AFTER HIGH SCHOOL: AN OVERVIEW FOR STUDENTS," BY PATRICA H. LATHAM, FROM THE LEARNING DISABILITIES ASSOCIATION OF AMERICA

DO THE LEGAL RIGHTS OF STUDENTS WITH LEARNING DISABILITIES CONTINUE AFTER HIGH SCHOOL?

Legal rights may continue. It depends upon the facts in the individual case. Children with learning disabilities who receive services under the Individuals with Disabilities Education Act (IDEA) or the Rehabilitation Act of 1973 (RA) in public elementary and secondary school may continue to have legal rights under federal laws in college programs and in employment. When students graduate from high school or reach age 21, their rights under the IDEA come to an end.

The rights that may continue are those under the Rehabilitation Act and the Americans with Disabilities Act of 1990 (ADA). To understand which rights continue, it is important to understand the three basic federal statutes that confer rights on people with disabilities.

The IDEA, initially enacted in 1975, provides for special education and related services for children with disabilities who need such education and services by reason of their disabilities. The IDEA provides for a Free Appropriate Public Education (FAPE) and for an Individualized Education Program (IEP).

The Rehabilitation Act, most notably Section 504, prohibits discrimination against children and adults with disabilities. The Rehabilitation Act applies to public and private elementary and secondary schools and colleges that receive federal funding. It also applies to employers that receive federal funding.

The ADA prohibits discrimination against children and adults with disabilities and applies to all public and most private schools and colleges, to testing entities, and to licensing authorities, regardless of federal funding. Religiously controlled educational institutions are exempt from coverage. The ADA applies to private employers with 15 or more employees and to state and local governments.

It may help to consider an example of how rights may continue over many years. Jeff has a reading disorder. For a long time he wanted to become a lawyer, and now he is in law school. He received special education and related services under the IDEA during public elementary school. He went to a small private religious high school and received accommodations under Section 504 of the Rehabilitation Act. He received extra test time on the SAT, during college, on the law school admission test (LSAT), and in law school. Under the ADA, he will be entitled to extra test time on the Bar Examination.

DO ALL PEOPLE WITH LEARNING DISABILITIES HAVE LEGAL RIGHTS UNDER THE REHABILITATION ACT AND ADA?

No. Many have legal rights, but some do not. Under the Rehabilitation Act and ADA, a disability is an impairment that substantially limits a major life activity, such as learning. Children and adults with learning disabilities, in many cases, have been found to have an impairment that substantially limits learning. That substantial limitation means that these individuals have a disability under the Rehabilitation Act and ADA and are protected under these laws.

Let's look at an example. Jim was diagnosed with a reading disorder and math disorder when he was six years old. He received special education under the IDEA for most of elementary school to assist with reading and math. By the time he entered high school, his reading comprehension and speed tested as average, but he continued to receive services under the IDEA for his math disorder through the end of high school. After graduation, Jim enrolled in art school. The art school required one math course as a requirement for graduation, but had a policy allowing course substitutions for the math requirement for students with disabilities that interfered with math. Jim disclosed his math disorder, requested a course substitution for math, and submitted good professional documentation of his disability and his need for accommodation.

WHAT RIGHTS DO I HAVE UNDER THE REHABILITATION ACT AND ADA AS A PERSON WITH A DISABILITY?

Basically you have the right to be free from discrimination on the basis of a disability. In the early school years, a child may be found ineligible under the IDEA but eligible under Section 504 and the ADA. The child would then receive services and accommodations under these anti-discrimination laws. In college, the Rehabilitation Act and ADA provide a right to accommodations for qualified persons with disabilities, so that courses, examinations, and activities will be accessible.

These laws also require reasonable accommodations in the workplace for qualified individuals with disabilities.

Notice that the protections of these laws are for qualified persons with disabilities. This means you must be qualified to do the college program or job in order to be protected under the law. You may have to prove you are qualified. This is different from public elementary and secondary school, where you were presumed to be qualified to be educated.

An example will illustrate this point. Karen had a reading disorder, auditory processing and memory retrieval problems. She received special education throughout public school. She had extra time on the SAT and did well enough to get into a college social work program. She disclosed her disabilities, requested the accommodation of extra test time and a reader for examinations, and provided supporting professional documentation. She received the requested accommodations but failed essay tests anyway. She was dismissed from the social work program. She then sought to set aside the dismissal on the ground that she couldn't take essay tests on such complex material because of her memory retrieval problem. In the end, the finding was that the school had provided all requested accommodations, that the school had done nothing improper, and that Karen was not qualified for the program.

WHAT ACCOMMODATIONS WOULD I BE ENTITLED TO IN COLLEGE?

College accommodations depend upon your particular disabilities and how they impact on you in the college setting. Accommodations might include: course accommodations (e.g., taped textbooks, use of a tape recorder, instructions orally and in writing, note taker, and priority seating) and examination accommodations (e.g., extended test time, reader, and quiet room).

WHAT ACCOMMODATIONS WOULD I BE ENTITLED TO IN MY JOB?

Workplace accommodations depend upon your particular disabilities and how they impact on performing the essential functions of your job. Accommodations might include: instructions orally and in writing, frequent and specific feedback from supervisors, quiet workspace, and training course accommodations.

WHAT ABOUT ADHD? IS IT COVERED UNDER THE LAW?

Yes, if it meets the criteria of the particular law. ADHD, while not expressly listed, may be covered by the IDEA under one of three categories: other health impairments, specific learning disabilities, and serious emotional disturbance. ADD has been found to be an impairment under the Rehabilitation Act and ADA and, like learning disabilities, is a disability if it substantially limits a major life activity, such as learning.

HOW DO I ASSERT MY RIGHTS IN COLLEGE?

You need to disclose your disability to the college, request specific accommodations, and supply supporting professional documentation. In public school, the school system has a duty to identify students with disabilities. This is not so in college. The student has the responsibility to disclose the disability and to request accommodations. You must be specific about the accommodations that you need because of your disability. It is not enough to say that you have learning disabilities, so the college must help you.

Let's look at an example. Sarah is taking courses at the community college. She has a reading disorder, expressive writing disorder, and ADD. She requested one and one-half time on tests, separate room for tests, a reader to read exam questions to her, and a scribe to take down her answers. She provided good professional documentation to support her request and was granted the requested accommodations.

There are student requests that the college is not obligated to grant. For example, if you did not request an accommodation on a test and failed it, generally you may not require the college to eliminate the failure from your record.

SHOULD I DISCLOSE MY DISABILITY AT WORK?

It depends If you do not need accommodations in the application process; generally it is best to wait until after you have the job. Once on the job, if you see that a part of your job is a problem for you and believe you need an accommodation, it is best to act promptly and not allow a long period of poor performance. Also, at the time you disclose your disability, request the specific reasonable accommodations that will enable you to do your job.

Let's consider an example. Carlos has problems with expressive writing, spelling, and fine motor coordination. After high school, he was hired as a security guard. On the job, he began to have problems with the reports he had to write. The reports were messy, had spelling errors, and were often submitted late. He sensed that his boss was becoming annoyed. Carlos disclosed his disabilities and requested that he be able dictate his reports into his tape recorder and then type them up on one of the computers (with spell check) at the main office at the end of each day. His request was granted.

HOW SHOULD I DISCLOSE MY DISABILITY?

Disclose the disability in writing. Be confident and positive. Combine the disclosure with a request for accommodations that will enable you to perform the job. Provide professional documentation of your disability and need for accommodations.

What documentation of my disability and need for accommodations do I have to provide?

You need to provide documentation that establishes that you have a disability and that you need the accommodations you have requested. This might be a letter or report for the college or employer from the professional who has evaluated you. It should state the diagnosis and tests and methods used in the diagnostic process, evaluate how the impairment impacts on you, and recommend reasonable accommodations.

WHAT IF I FIND OUT I HAVE A LEARNING DISABILITY DURING COLLEGE OR EVEN LATER?

A late diagnosis of learning disabilities may be questioned more than an early diagnosis. It is important to have excellent documentation of the disability. It may be important to explain why the disability was not evident earlier. For example, Janet was diagnosed during her first year of college with a reading disorder. There were reasons why the problem had not shown up earlier. She had done well in the elementary and secondary school because she went to schools that did not have timed tests. She put in the extra time needed to successfully complete her course work and her tests. In college, timed tests posed a major problem for her and led her to seek a thorough evaluation. She was able to document her reading disorder and her need for extra test time in college and medical school.

WHAT IF I TAKE MEDICATION FOR ADD? DO I STILL HAVE RIGHTS?

Yes. The existence of a disability is to be judged without reference to the possible beneficial effects of medication. The taking of prescription medication for ADD does not result in loss of disability status under the Rehabilitation Act and ADA or in loss of reasonable accommodations.

CAN LEARNING DISABILITIES OR ADD CAUSE A PERSON TO BE REJECTED FOR SERVICE IN THE ARMED FORCES?

It depends. Many individuals with learning disabilities or ADD join the Armed Forces and report that the structure and clear expectations help them to do well. However, these conditions may prevent some individuals from obtaining the required score on the Armed Forces Qualifying Test. The Armed Forces are not required to grant accommodations, such as extended test time, on the qualifying test. Further, military regulations provide that academic skills deficits that interfere with school or work after the age of 12 may be a cause for rejection for service in the Armed Forces. These regulations also provide that current use of medication, such as Ritalin or Dexedrine, to improve academic skills is disqualifying for military service.

CAN I BE FIRED FROM MY JOB OR DISMISSED FROM COLLEGE EVEN IF I ESTABLISH THAT I HAVE A DISABILITY?

Yes. Having a disability does not create absolute entitlement to a job or college education. The purpose of the anti-discrimination laws is to make sure you have equal opportunity. For example, if you have math disorder and cannot pass a required math course (with no substitutions permitted) for an engineering program, then you would not be qualified for the engineering program.

WHAT ABOUT CONFIDENTIALITY OF DISABILITY RECORDS I FILE WITH A COLLEGE OR AN EMPLOYER?

Colleges generally have confidentiality policies with respect to disability material. The employment provisions of the ADA contain confidentiality provisions. However, these provisions are not as strong as the IDEA provision that provides for a right to delete disability records contained in your public school files.

For example, Ruth's parents submitted professional documentation of her learning disabilities and depression to her public high school. Ruth submitted the same documentation to her first employer when she disclosed her disabilities and requested job accommodations. After leaving her first job and being hired by a new employer, Ruth decided that she did not need accommodations in the new job. She also decided to request deletion of her disability information from prior files, while retaining copies in her own files in case she would need the records later. The public high school complied with her request. Her first employer informed her that the disability information could not be deleted but was kept in a separate, confidential file.

IF I DON'T GET WHAT I ASK FOR, SHOULD I SUE?

A lawsuit is not the first step. First, you must evaluate your own position. It may be wise to consult with a lawyer to review the strong points and weak points in your case. If your case has merit, and you wish to pursue it, then follow these steps: communicate to the college or employer the basic facts and the reasons why you are entitled to what you have requested, negotiate by marshaling the facts that support your request, consider alternative dispute resolution (e.g., mediation and arbitration), and finally consider formal proceedings, such as litigation in the courts.

Remember, even if you have a strong case, it does not mean you must take legal action. You may decide that you wish to put your energy into moving on to a new college program or job rather than disputing events at the prior program.

1. What are the important rights that students with disabilities have in college?

2. What legal recourse might students have if they are not given such accommodations?

"HANDLING OBJECTIONS" BY AFRICA S. HANDS, FROM *SUCCESSFULLY SERVING THE COLLEGE BOUND*, PUBLISHED BY THE AMERICAN LIBRARY ASSOCIATION, DECEMBER 24, 2014

You may face objections to your plans to increase or start specific services and programs for college-bound members of your community even though it is supported by the data presented in chapter 1. National data supporting college enrollment trends may not be sufficient to generate support from your library's administration and your colleagues. The national data show that the immediate college enrollment rate for high-school completers has increased over the years. But what does that mean for Louisville, Kentucky, or Oakland, California? You may need to present micro-level data on your own city, county, or state, and use other research and examples to bolster your case. The United States Census Bureau's American FactFinder website (http://factfinder2.census.gov) provides city-level data that can be used along with county-level data to illustrate your community's standing.[1] Your state's Department of Education should also have enrollment data and trend information (if only for traditional-age college-bound students).

Because you may also face other questions or objections, you will need to prepare for these conversations.

Preparation, research, and the results of your needs assessment will demonstrate to administrators and colleagues that you invested considerable time and thought into your plans, and that you understand that it may take time to build a steady audience for this new programming.

Starting out with only a few programs to help your college-bound patrons is better than nothing at all. This chapter addresses some questions or concerns you may encounter when implementing these programs.

OBJECTION #1

"Our patrons already know how to research and apply for college. We see them do it all the time."

RESPONSE

It is true that you have many college-bound patrons who are proactive and informed, and know the ropes when it comes to higher education and college planning. The US Census Bureau may report that the college-going population includes people of all ages. However, because you may only see young adults, your programs may be geared toward traditional college-bound patrons. You can support your older students by adding programs to suit their needs (as revealed in needs-assessment interviews). As a librarian at an institution that must serve the information, cultural, and educational needs of the community, you support the regular activities of your current patrons. You also have a duty to anticipate the needs of your potential (and possibly less knowledgeable) patrons by highlighting programs they may not expect to find at the library.

Those patrons need services and programs to help them reach their higher education and vocational goals. By introducing new programs and expanding existing ones, making them more visible through increased promotion, and publicizing them to a variety of patrons, you simultaneously serve your current patrons, and welcome those more infrequent users—particularly adult and nontraditional students—who may not be aware of all the library has to offer, or who may be reluctant to ask for help.

OBJECTION #2

"We are not college counselors."

RESPONSE

You have experience adapting to changing patron needs. You have the skills, intelligence, and creativity necessary to get up to speed on a topic and provide patrons with information and resources to satisfy their needs. (For example, those of you who were not well-versed in the functions of e-readers and iPads several years ago now use them to conduct on-the-spot tutorials and similar programs for patrons.) Additionally, many of you have attended, or currently may be attending college, and can draw on that experience to assist patrons. Your goal is not to become college counselors or advisors, but to serve the various information needs of the college-bound community, just as you would for other groups.

As with any information services, we do not plan to advise patrons which specific courses of action to take, but rather to help them to find information about college planning. An analogy would be the role of libraries in helping patrons during the introduction of the Affordable Care Act (ACA). Though most of us are not health-care experts or medical librarians, when the ACA was introduced, the staffs of libraries across the United States helped patrons to access reputable, unbiased information about the Act and state-level marketplace exchanges, and to "respond to other questions of fact related to changes in coverage and care mandated by the Act."[2] This included setting up information pages on the library's website with links to official information, resources, and forms. For example, the Montana State Library created a library learning portal with resources for library staff.[3]

Librarians do not need to become experts in higher education, but they should be able to share information about a range of print and online resources, general deadlines, and academic programs offered at local colleges and universities to meet basic and moderately specialized information needs.

OBJECTION #3

"Aren't schools providing this information?"

RESPONSE

Some high schools provide comprehensive college counseling and preparation programs. Schools with high college-enrollment rates often have counseling staffs that spend more than 50 percent of their time on college counseling.[4] Schools whose counselors devote significant amounts of time to the details of preparing and selecting colleges and applying for financial aid show an increase in the percentage of students who attend college. Some schools also have lower counselor-to-student ratios that allow for more interaction with the student body. In one study, the counselor-to-student ratio at private high schools was 1 to 106, compared to 1 to 299 for public high schools.[5] However, low counselor-to-student ratios are not the reality in many school districts.

Although the American School Counselor Association (ASCA) recommends a counselor-to-student ratio of 1 to 250, the average ratio for the entire United States was 1 to 471 during academic year 2010–2011. Average ratios may be lower in individual states. According to ASCA, California's was 1 to 1,016 in the year studied.[6]

Although some college-bound students are indeed receiving services and programs from their schools, many others are not, due to limited funding, staffing and a focus on other pressing issues. Coupled with an unreasonable volume of students to counsel, counselors work with students on complicated day-to-day issues that compete with college planning: truancy and behavioral issues, violence in the home, homelessness, poverty, high-stakes testing, and learning disabilities. Counselors and students need all the supplemental support they can get to direct students toward a college education.

OBJECTION #4

"What about school libraries?"

RESPONSE

"Woodworking and foreign language teachers, library staff and social worker among 10 job cuts proposed to balance Rockland-area school budget."[7]

"ICCSD teacher librarians facing fallout from cuts."[8]
"Many L.A. Unified school libraries, lacking staff, are forced to shut."[9]

These are recent headlines about the state of school libraries. Some school libraries are on the verge of extinction. As with school counselors, school librarians and staff may wish to provide programs and support for college-bound students, but their hands are already full. They are fighting a battle merely to survive, let alone support a variety of programs for college-bound students. Also keep in mind that your population of college-bound patrons is not limited to youth who may get services in school. Because your audience is broad, so should be your information services and programs. Though you might like to depend on others to provide college-planning services, because that is not the reality, the need is ever present.

OBJECTION #5

"Our library cannot afford to serve another special population."

RESPONSE

Your library can't afford *not* to serve potential college students. As discussed in chapter 1, a college degree not only increases employment chances but also an individual's overall quality of life—health outcomes, civic involvement, and job satisfaction—which benefits the community at large. Keep in mind that these programs and services do not exist in a vacuum. To start or increase programs, the library will need to seek partnerships with other community agencies and funding from outside sources while working to increase their own funding.

The Phoenix Library's College Depot was started with seed money from a grant that was used to hire a contract staff member and form an advisory committee. That contract fundraiser raised nearly $1 million. The goal was to raise enough funds to operate for a few years, prove the program's worth, and then seek additional funds from the city and other supporters. The College Depot also has a thirteen-member advisory committee with members from the Arizona Department of Education, local colleges, the Phoenix Union High School District, and United Way.[10]

The Free Library of Philadelphia received financial support from the Christian R. and Mary F. Lindback Foundation and the Dolfinger-McMahon Foundation to offer comprehensive college-planning services.[11] Both foundations are located in the library's home state of Pennsylvania, but similar funding sources and partners may be available in your city and state.

The Great Lakes Higher Education Corporation is an example of such a partner. It funds projects that prepare more students to enroll and succeed in college-level courses. The goal of the 2014–2015 grant was to "help more high school juniors and seniors and adult learners avoid the need for developmental education."[12] Previous grant recipients proposed programs similar to those described in chapter 5: ACT workshops and tutoring, exposure to guest speakers, college tours, and other academic support. Unfortunately, libraries were not on the list of its recent recipients.

These seemingly "non-library" activities can be provided by libraries that have an interest in actively engaging college-bound patrons. The library is not expected to be the sole provider of college-planning resources in the community; there are other agencies and organizations that do similar work. Although it will not be the main program provider, the library can certainly collaborate with others who have similar interests and have received funding. There is funding available for college-readiness programs. The funding source may not be library-related, and past funding recipients may not have been libraries. Still, the money is out there to serve college-bound patrons. Remember, there is no need to rush; you can add programs over time as you build your college-bound audience and increase funding sources.

With library cuts in school districts and yet more for already overworked school counselors, public libraries, which are information providers in the community can overcome these objections by training already skilled and knowledgeable staff and with the aid of local partners.

1. What does the author present as the community's role in getting students ready for college?

2. How might these resources help with the college admissions process?

"THE FOR-PROFIT COLLEGE SCAM: WHY I SUPPORT THE DEBT STRIKE AGAINST MY FORMER EMPLOYER," BY DAWN LUECK, FROM *COMMON DREAMS*, MAY 8, 2015

This spring, around 100 indebted college grads came up with a novel strategy for dealing with their crushing debt: They simply weren't going to pay it.

These students — the so-called "Corinthian 100— attended schools owned by the now-defunct for-profit education conglomerate Corinthian Colleges.

With over 100 campuses in the United States and Canada, Corinthian's schools — including Everest and Heald College campuses, among others — offered "career-oriented" degrees in fields such as nursing, business, criminal justice, and information technology.

Since at least 2007, the company has been under investigation by various state and federal agencies for pushing students into high-interest loans and defrauding them with false promises of high-paying careers.

I'm a former corporate finance manager for Corinthian — and I support the debt strikers. I agree with the Debt Collective, a grassroots organization with which I'm affiliated, that the federal government should cancel Corinthian students' loans.

Most students at for-profit colleges like Corinthian are targeted because of their vulnerable circumstances. They have dire financial needs and, because they're often the first in their families to attend college, they don't have the kind of knowledge and experience about college admissions that wealthier students do.

They're lured in by salespeople disguised as helpful admissions officials, who offer students a convenient schedule — along with empty promises of higher earnings and a better life. What students get instead is a lifetime of debt and a worthless degree.

Before Corinthian outsourced my job to another company in 2012, I helped develop some of those recruitment techniques. I know firsthand that the industry is designed to desensitize employees to the human cost of what they're doing.

Through high-pressure micromanagement tactics — such as evaluating employee performance based on the number of students recruited — Corinthian employees were encouraged to hide facts about the school that would have turned prospective students away.

Once a student signs the enrollment agreement, he or she is basically reduced to a student ID number in the minds of campus leaders and corporate executives.

Does this number come with grant funding? How many loan dollars does this number represent, and how much profit?

That's the kind of information management demands from admissions representatives and financial aid administrators on a weekly basis. The needs of the student are thrown out the window.

When students become nothing but a number, it's easier to take advantage of them.

Tens of billions in federal student aid has flowed into for-profit college coffers and into investor pockets over the last two decades. It's the students who are left on the hook.

As a result of this relentless drive for profit, Corinthian students ended up borrowing more than they intended and often misunderstood the amount they would owe after graduation. That's no accident: The process was designed to be easily misunderstood.

The federal government and state authorities have investigated for-profit colleges for years.

Earlier this year, the Department of Education helped Corinthian sell some of its failing schools, preventing some currently enrolled students from getting a debt discharge. When student debt strikers brought the issue to national attention, Corinthian was forced to shut down its remaining campuses.

So far, the Department of Education has failed to give defrauded students the relief they deserve. Instead, these colleges' manipulative tactics have left hundreds of thousands of people buried in debt for worthless degrees.

This predatory system takes a toll on employees as well as students. The relentless demand to meet recruitment targets resulted in anxiety-related health problems for many of my former coworkers.

I commend the Corinthian 100 for fighting back. I hope other current and former Corinthian employees will take inspiration from them and come forward to tell the truth about the for-profit college scam.

1. What does the author feel for-profit schools are doing to students?

2. What has the government done to confront for-profit schools and hold them accountable? How should students protect themselves from predatory institutions?

"A NATION AT RISK—HOW GIFTED, LOW-INCOME KIDS ARE LEFT BEHIND," BY JONATHAN WAI AND FRANK C. WORRELL, FROM *THE CONVERSATION* WITH THE PARTNERSHIP OF THE UNIVERSITY OF CALIFORNIA, MARCH 21, 2016

In 1983, the National Commission on Excellence in Education published *A Nation At Risk: The Imperative for Educational Reform*, which documented widespread academic underachievement at every level, concluding:

"For the first time in the history of our country, the educational skills of one generation will not surpass, will not equal, will not even approach, those of their parents."

In 1996, education researchers Camilla Benbow and Julian Stanley published a paper reviewing decades of evidence showing the achievement of students with high intellectual potential had markedly declined, building upon *A Nation at Risk* by arguing:

"Our nation's brightest youngsters, those most likely to be headed for selective colleges, have suffered dramatic setbacks over the past two decades. This has grave implications for our country's ability to compete economically with other industrialized nations."

One of their key points was that the federal education K-12 budget allocated a mere 0.0002 percent for "gifted and talented education," programs targeted at helping the most academically advanced students develop their talents.

Fast forward another two decades. In a paper just published in the journal *Policy Insights from the Behavioral and Brain Sciences*, we document that this rate has not changed at all. In the 2015 federal education budget of US$49.8 billion, gifted and talented education accounted for 0.0002 percent. In other words, for every $500,000 spent, only a single dollar was allocated for gifted education.

This consistent lack of investment in gifted kids for decades has created a deep divide between the educational, occupational and leadership attainment of low-income and high-income students.

As researchers of gifted education, we believe this has significant implications not only for the well-being of these disadvantaged students, but also for societal innovation and even America's GDP.

THE CRITICAL K-12 YEARS

A 2007 Jack Kent Cooke Foundation research study shows talented low-income students as a whole are not achieving their full potential.

Despite initially being academically talented, these students fall out of the high-achieving group during their K-12 school years. They rarely rise into the ranks of the highest achievers. Very few ever graduate from college or go on to graduate school.

This study, which defined high-achieving as the top 25 percent of students in U.S. schools, estimated that 3.4 million gifted students from lower-income families are underachieving due to a lack of opportunity.

Another study – from economists Caroline Hoxby and Christopher Avery – defined high-achieving as the top 4 percent of U.S. high school students. Here it was estimated that 35,000 low-income gifted students are underperforming.

These numbers reveal the importance of the K-12 education years. For that is when talented students from all backgrounds can be identified and given support.

It's hard to develop talent properly if you don't identify it early. A key part of the problem is that gifted low-income students are not being identified systematically. Typically, parents or teachers nominate individual kids as gifted. These kids are then tested and placed in educational programming that matches their ability.

Consequently, the identification of gifted children is sometimes left to the discretion of parents and teachers, which could leave out some low-income and minority children.

Another part of the problem is that while financially advantaged students can access opportunities outside of school to develop their talent, financially disadvantaged students rely on public education programs to develop their talent.

If such public K-12 funding is near zero, it should be no surprise that these students fail to receive the consistent educational stimulation needed to achieve at the levels they are capable of.

This is despite the fact that research from the field of gifted education has documented the impact of educational programs targeted at low-income students.

IMPACT ON COLLEGE ADMISSIONS

The cumulative disadvantage that low-income kids face through K-12 then carries over in higher education, which is why we see deep divides at this stage of the educational pipeline.

High-achieving low-income kids are less likely to apply to elite schools.

Education researchers Michael Bastedo and Ozan Jaquette, who analyzed decades of data, found that only 0.4 percent of students in the lowest socioeconomic group attended "most competitive" schools in 1972 and only 0.5 percent in 2004. Contrast this with students from the top socioeconomic group – 5.2 percent of them attended "most competitive" schools in 1972 and 6.2 percent in 2004.

This shows that low-income students are largely underrepresented and have not increased their representation at the most selective institutions.

Additional research shows low-income high-achieving students are less likely to apply to top schools. This is largely due to these students not having the academic preparation required for selective institutions. Given the intense competition involved in elite college admissions, it takes years of preparation and resources to be competitive for these colleges.

The truth is that students who end up in elite schools, by and large, are not ordinary when it comes to academic talent. In fact, they are largely in the top few percentiles of the population. And no matter what varied individual admission policies are used by each school, research by one of us shows that top scorers end up in elite schools.

In other words, elite college education is largely gifted education.

But for decades it has served as gifted or advanced education for those highly talented students who come from financially advantaged backgrounds, whose parents have devoted years of resources toward the goal of elite college admission.

IMPACT ON LEADERSHIP, INNOVATION AND GDP

Elite schools largely feed positions of national and global leadership. As research by one of us shows, over half of the people who currently hold positions of leadership and power in our society have attended elite schools.

So, this lack of support for gifted low-income kids has consequences for their representation in positions of leadership in society as well as lost innovations.

As we argue in our recent paper, for at least the last half-century, we have underserved low-income gifted kids, losing countless minds and corresponding innovations.

Research from the Study of Mathematically Precocious Youth, led by David Lubinski and Camilla Benbow, shows that fully developed gifted students earn doctorates and university tenure, publish fiction and nonfiction books and register patents at rates two to eight times higher than the general population. Other research too shows that gifted students have a long-term impact on GDP.

This is further corroborated by the work done by Nobel Prize-winning economist James Heckman showing that investing in students early can have a long-term economic and societal payoff and that investment in higher-ability students has a higher payoff.

Based on a synthesis of the evidence, we believe a policy focus on identifying and challenging disadvantaged students early on would contribute to leveling the playing field, fulfilling their talent and increasing their well-being. Testing all students, rather than relying on the traditional parent/teacher nomination system, will actually serve as a tool for greater fairness in placing low-income and minority students in the gifted programming they need. A small early investment in these talented students would pay off in intellectual and technological innovations, as well as GDP, benefiting us all.

As Thomas Jefferson wrote in Notes on the State of Virginia:

"By that part of our plan which prescribes the selection of the youths of genius from among the classes of the poor, we hope to avail the state of those talents which nature has sown as liberally among the poor as the rich, but which perish without use, if not sought for and cultivated."

1. According to the research presented here, why are low-income students overlooked by admissions teams?

2. What can be done at all stages of the education system to make sure all students are given an equal opportunity?

"GEORGE WASHINGTON UNIVERSITY HAS FOR YEARS CLAIMED TO BE 'NEED-BLIND.' IT'S NOT," BY MARIAN WANG, FROM *PROPUBLICA*, OCTOBER 22, 2013

George Washington University — which got in trouble last year for misreporting admissions data to bolster its college ranking — is making yet another confession.

The university has been misrepresenting its admissions and financial-aid policy for years, touting a "need-blind" admissions policy while in fact giving preference to wealthier students in the final stages of the admissions process, according to the student newspaper, the GW Hatchet, which first reported on the practice. Meanwhile, hundreds of academically comparable but needier students were put on the waitlist for admission because they lacked the financial resources.

Many colleges and universities like to tout "need-blind" admissions processes, or the practice of judging their applicants' academic qualifications strictly on their merits and making decisions without factoring in applicants' wealth. In recent years, some colleges that have traditionally been need-blind have weighed whether to become more need-aware.

Until a few days ago, the undergraduate admissions page for George Washington University stated, "Requests for financial aid do not affect admissions decisions." That language was removed over the weekend. (Here's the archived version.) [*Editor's note: Please find links with the original article.*]

The updated page now explains that the admissions committee "evaluates" candidates initially without factoring in their financial need, but then considers applicants' financial resources "at the point of finalizing admissions decisions."

"I believe using the phrase 'need aware' better represents the totality of our practices than using the phrase 'need blind,'" Laurie Koehler, senior associate provost for enrollment management, said in a statement to ProPublica.

"What we are trying to do is increase the transparency of the admissions process," said Koehler.

Top GW administrators have repeatedly stated over the years that the university is need-blind. When the student newspaper in 2011 did a story about how some colleges are moving away from need-blind admissions, one administrator told the paper, "We're still need-blind."

It's worth noting that the "need-blind" label can be as much about marketing as it is about giving all applicants a fair shot.

Many schools are "need-blind" but don't actually give out much need-based aid. We recently detailed how universities, looking to boost their bottom lines, are increasingly using financial-aid dollars to attract wealthier students.

"It sounds better to people to say, 'We're need-blind.' People think that's a badge of courage," said Matt Malatesta, vice president for admissions, financial aid, and enrollment at Union College, a small liberal arts college in New York that practices need-aware admissions.

Unless schools pony up the aid dollars to meet students' financial needs, touting the need-blind label isn't particularly meaningful for students, who may simply get the offer of admission along with an offer to take on unsustainable debt.

"There are pluses and minuses on both sides of the debate," Malatesta said in an earlier interview. "I'm not a believer that one is better than another."

But in contrast to GW, many of the schools that have weighed the pluses and minuses of need-blind versus need-aware have done so quite publicly.

Grinnell College, for instance, announced earlier this year that after considering whether to become need-aware, it would remain need-blind for the time being -- but would still look to wealthier students in the recruitment process and use merit aid to help attract them.

Wesleyan University last year took the other route, announcing it would give up the "need-blind" label and start to consider students' financial need once its aid dollars were given out.

Both institutions are part of a handful of colleges across the country that promise to meet the full needs of all admitted students. George Washington University has not offered any such guarantee.

Earlier this year, George Washington University was featured in the *Washington Post* as trying to buck its "rich-kid reputation." "I'm not going to deny we have a lot of students that come from wealthy families," GW President Steven Knapp told the *Post* in April. "But we are increasingly trying to diversify, and I think we have been diversifying compared to where we were 10 years ago."

About 13 percent of undergraduates at George Washington University receive the federal Pell grant for low-income students. That's low, according to a recent report by the New America Foundation that also noted that the university charges its few low-income students, on average, a high net price even after grants and scholarships.

Tuition alone is more than $47,000 a year, and room and board costs another $11,000. The majority of students at the university pay less than the full sticker price, due to the university's strategy of offering grants as discounts.

But even after grants are applied, low-income students at GW still pay a heavy price. Federal data for the 2011-2012 school year show that students at the university coming from families making $30,000 or less paid, on average, $21,000 to attend the university.

1. What are need-blind universities and colleges?

2. Why is it important that institutions are accessible for applicants from different economic backgrounds?

"IS THERE A VIABLE ALTERNATIVE TO COLLEGE?" BY JEFFREY TUCKER, FROM THE FOUNDATION FOR ECONOMIC EDUCATION, JULY 18, 2013

During a recent conference, a man around 50 pulled me over to the side. He said he had a serious question to ask me about his daughter's education. I said, "of course," but I already suspected what the question was, because I've been asked it a hundred times.

"I'm preparing to spend some $100,000-plus on my daughter's college education, and that's despite loans and scholarships. It's a major financial strain. I want her to succeed, but my fear is that the cost is not worth it. What do you think?"

It's not so easy just to say yes. Or to say no. When it is your kid's life, this decision could be epic, and the results of your choice could echo in this world long after you are gone. This is why parents start feeling terrible anxiety over college from the time their child enters high school. The scramble for scholarships, the pressure on standardized tests, the push for a maniacal academic focus—it all defines the teen years. This angst ends up causing terrible family tensions and seems to punish kids for just wanting to be kids.

And even if the teen does everything right—every test trained for and taken five times, every activity listed on the portfolio, a high GPA, top of the class, early applications and admissions—you are not home free. You are going to spend six figures, but there is also a high opportunity cost: you remove your child from remunerative work for four years, and this is after four years of no employment in high school. That means both lost income and lost job experience. College is costly in every way.

Meanwhile, the job market is tight in ways that previous generations have never known. Fear of new health-care mandates makes companies reluctant to take the risk on full timers. The Association of Graduate Recruiters reports that jobs available for new graduates will fall by 4 percent again this year, with 85 applicants for every 1 job available. Government has been cracking down on internships and they are very hard to come by.

A chilling survey from Reuters shows that 42 percent of existing college graduates are underemployed, meaning part-time work and few opportunities to expand. A third are $30,000 in debt, and 17 percent owe up to $50,000. Only half of those who find full-time work are actually employed in their field of study. Some 40 percent of those surveyed believe that they will have to spend more time and more money on an advanced degree to get the job they really want.

But even then there are no guarantees except for the sheer cost of this gamble. Unemployment among 20–24-year-olds is actually slightly higher this year over last—the only demographic for which this is true. Among this group, the unemployment rate (according to the narrowest measure) is 13.2 percent—a figure that would cause national panic if it applied to adults. Most of these kids have a safety net called parents.

You don't need the surveys to tell you any of this bad news. When the parents of today's late teens were that age, the world was their oyster (which they "with sword would open"). They didn't worry. They didn't think that much about jobs while in college or after. They could take time off and follow the Grateful Dead, languish in European backpack travels, take temporary positions they could easily quit, or anything else. They could pretty much take a job they wanted at a time of their choosing.

The world is completely different today and parents know this. The results of 50 years of government programs that pushed higher education as the ticket to happiness and prosperity are in—and they don't look good. The massive loans, subsidies, and incentives didn't make people in general smarter and richer. They just diverted resources and squeezed out private alternatives.

Cracks are starting to show in the entire apparatus that government built. Now, at mid-summer, while preparing for school to start again, millions of parents are seriously vexed about their children's future and especially about the tremendous problem of college costs. No one knows for sure if it is a good choice, but the risk of foregoing college altogether is too high.

The data bear this out, too. Workers without college degrees earn on average about 60 percent of what a college graduate earns. And there are other chilling correlations, such as how two-thirds of the prison population is made up of people without college degrees. It's a fallacy to confuse correlation with causation, but nevertheless such facts give one pause about foregoing higher education altogether.

It's no surprise that parents end up coughing up even at tremendous financial sacrifice. Parents would gladly step in front of a bus to save their children, so facing debt and financial loss for a few years seems just part of parental obligation. This is why, in economic terms, the demand for college is relatively inelastic: Parents keep paying and paying no matter how bad it gets.

(As an aside, America has a very strange education system, once you think about it. People presume that all education from first to twelfth grade should be "free of charge" as a human right, but one year of formal education after that should cost the fullness of an average family income!)

For how long will people bear this tremendous cost without demanding some alternatives?

The other day at lunch, I saw a hint of how the present situation might change in the future. I was talking to a very talented graphic-design artist and I asked him about his college education. He said that he dropped out after his sophomore year to take a job in the industry.

He explained: "I couldn't take the risk of not being employed after graduation. In my field, the employers regard college as evidence that you are willing to waste lots of time and money doing not much of anything productive. I decided to gain the competitive advantage and jump into the workforce at the age of 20, get experience, and start climbing the ladder."

That set me back a pace or two. I had expected that we would start to see this happening in the future, that at some point employers would regard a college degree as a liability, as evidence that a person has few skills and a high sense of entitlement. But to meet someone who had already acted on this scenario was intriguing.

Here's my prediction: We are going to see the emergence of more credible one- and two-year alternatives to college. These programs will combine real work experience with rigorous learning and cost a small fraction of what college costs. It can't work for some professions like law and medicine, mainly because of government controls and guild-like admissions certifications. But in fields like technology, design, and business, this seems like a great idea.

Sound good? I know of two such programs now.

One is Enstitute, a two-year program that focuses on real skills and apprenticeships with tech companies and non-profits. It's already difficult to gain admission given the flood of applications.

Another institution takes this idea and adds a liberal-arts focus, which seems like a great idea. It's called Praxis, and it is accepting its first batch of students for this fall. The program lasts 10 months, and, according to the website, can be treated as a college substitute, a pre-college program, or a post-college program.

"It's for entrepreneurial 18- to 25-year-olds who want real-world career experience and the best of online education all in one ... Don't get stuck choosing between the intellectual value of a humanities degree and the practical value of a business degree or work experience. Get it all."

Such programs directly address the number-one complaint that all employers report about new graduates: They are good at sitting in desks and that's about it. This is a serious problem. These innovative programs actually recall the types of apprenticeships that were common before the government decided that everyone should be stuck in school during the most productive years of their lives.

These programs smash the paradigm that's been around since after the Second World War. They are the grass growing up in the sidewalk cracks. Just as homeschooling changed the way we think of elementary and secondary schooling, combined work-and-study programs like Enstitute and Praxis might change the way we think about college forever.

It has to happen. For five hundred years, college was for philosophy, theology, history, and language, and a small percentage of the population attended following rigorous high school experiences. In the last 50 years, college has become the educator of everything while high school has become dominated by extracurricular concerns.

Can this change be reversed? As with the housing bubble, the trend will change when people perceive the costs as outweighing benefits and bail out. As this tendency grows, alternative programs will grow and thrive. The path toward a freer educational market will be paved by private entrepreneurial efforts to meet the human needs that government programs leave unserved.

1. According to the author, are there alternatives to college? What would an option need to be in order to be an alternative to college?

2. Should students have options other than college to open the door to new opportunities? Why or why not?

"IDEAS FROM ABROAD: REFORMING THE AUSTRALIAN UNIVERSITY ADMISSIONS SYSTEM," BY CLAIRE BROWN, FROM *THE CONVERSATION*, AUGUST 15, 2016

Following the government's decision to undertake consultations on how best to reform Australian higher education, one of the key areas up for debate is about how to create an effective university admissions system.

The value of the ATAR – where high school students receive an overall ranking that is often, although not solely, used as a way to select students for higher education courses – has been called into question. Vice-chancellors have called the model "meaningless" and "too simplistic". Some have even called for the model to be scrapped entirely.

There has been lots of discussion around whether the current model is working well. What are some alternatives?

Education is notorious for re-inventing the same policy wheels. With that in mind, let's take a look at some of the world's best-performing higher education systems to see what they do differently to give us some inspiration – and possible guidance.

THE USA – ELITE MODEL

The US has no overall national university entrance system. But there are some areas of commonality across the states in how a large number of universities – both public and private – select and admit students.

Generally, each university sets its admission requirements within state legislative requirements. This includes an indication of academic performance as demonstrated by performance on either the SAT or ACT – both standardized tests – and some demonstration of high school competencies based on specific subject combinations and levels of achievement in those subjects.

US universities typically provide opportunities for students to include information about their extracurricular activities to demonstrate their readiness for university. This may include evidence of leadership, service, work experience, motivation and personal experience.

Many universities also require or allow students to submit an essay or personal statement to further make their case for admission.

At Harvard University, where six out of every 100 applicants are accepted, the entrance requirements are demanding. Domestic and international applicants must complete the Common Application or Universal College Application. In addition, they must submit:

- Harvard College Questions for the Common Application or the Universal College Application Harvard supplement
- ACT with writing, or old SAT or new SAT with writing
- normally, 2 SAT subject tests
- school report and high school transcript
- two teacher reports
- mid-year school report
- final school report.

ALTERNATIVE MODEL TO HELP DISADVANTAGED STUDENTS ACCESS UNIVERSITY

The Early College High School models are an increasingly popular alternative pathway into university for underrepresented students.

This movement began in 2002 and was originally funded by the Bill and Melinda Gates Foundation and others to help students from disadvantaged and low-SES backgrounds aspire to and gain affordable access to university.

There are different models, but generally schools and universities partner to provide college classes replacing some of the traditional high-school classes. These may be delivered at the school or on the university campus.

Students who complete their Early College High School courses receive direct entry to the partner university and up to two years of college credit.

Findings from the American Institutes for Research 2013 Early College High School Initiative Impact Study found that:

Early College students had a greater opportunity than their peers to enrol in and graduate from college. They also appeared to be on a different academic trajectory, with Early College students earning college degrees and enrolling in four-year institutions at higher rates than comparison students. Early Colleges appeared to mitigate the traditional educational attainment gaps between advantaged and disadvantaged students.

THE UK

School-leaver applications to universities in England, Scotland, Wales and Northern Ireland are processed through the Universities and Colleges Admissions Service (UCAS). The majority of UK universities use the UCAS systems for both domestic and international undergraduate applicants.

UCAS requires students to submit their predicted grades, achievements, a cover letter outlining skills and

163

why they want to study that particular subject area. Some students will also be expected to do an admissions test and/or interview. Applicants submit their applications for up to five universities in order of preference.

Universities then make conditional or unconditional offers, sometimes based on the student meeting the required grades.

Students who don't meet the required grades set by the university can go through a process called "Clearing". This allows applicants to contact universities directly to plead their case for places that have yet to be filled. Clearing occurs largely over the phone on a set day – but the process can take weeks. It can be a brutal process, particularly for students still coming to terms with the fact that they didn't get in to their university of choice.

As many as half of the UK universities require students to sit their own, additional admissions tests as they are losing confidence in the A-level grades as an accurate indicator of students' academic capabilities. A greater diversity of students – more than 30% – are now entering through alternative pathways without A levels.

GERMANY

As in the US, responsibility for the education systems is state-based and applications are made directly to each university.

However, in Germany, higher education is free.

If candidates already have a European qualification, such as the Baccalaureate or A-levels, potential students may only be required to prove proficiency in German and/ or English depending on the course of study.

Previously, domestic students had to have completed a matriculation exam known as the Arbitur, which equates to the Baccalaureate or A-levels.

The Arbitur is losing its prominence as the defining entry point to German universities. Students are increasingly entering university via alternative pathways.

An essential difference in the German context requires an understanding of the school system.

From fourth grade, students are streamed into pathways that can determine their future academic options. Traditionally, it was students who completed the Gymnasium high school pathway (out of three potential pathways, the other two being Hauptschule and Realschule) who were specifically prepared for university entrance during year 12 or 13.

This explains why entry into university appears to be a little less demanding than other countries. The sifting and sorting process has occurred earlier, right back in primary school.

OPTIONS FOR AUSTRALIA

We have an opportunity. The most effective selection system to use will depend on what we are trying to accomplish with our higher education system. The question is what is our tertiary system most trying to do, and for whose benefit?

Like the rest of the world, we've massified and moved the focus to the private benefit of a university degree, creating an argument for users to pay more – private good versus public good.

The nature of the product has changed. When 40% of our population is getting a degree, the nature of what it is changes – as will the manner in which we select for it. This is a precursor for an analysis of how we should select students for entry.

The elites, who still have students banging on the door, want to leave the system as it is. They are taking the top 10-15%, as they have always done. Nothing's changed for them.

The difference is that in previous times only the top 10-15% went to university. ATAR is efficient for them; 95.70 you're in, 95.65 you're out. Why change?

The ones at the other end of the rankings competition want a different system, because their supply of students has dried up and the ATAR system is laying bare their weakness – there are no longer any students they won't take. They're looking for alternative admission systems because the current one delivers them no students.

The ones in the middle are hedging their bets.

That's the nub of the issue. There's no "best" system for Australia unless we know what we are trying to do. At the moment, the discussion is being driven by universities for self-interest, not for what's best for the country or the sector.

1. How does the US admissions system compare to other countries?

2. Should the United States look to other countries for ideas on how to reform the admissions system? Why or why not?

CHAPTER 5

WHAT THE MEDIA SAY

The media is where we see many of our society's most important questions being debated, developed, and decided. For higher education and college admissions, that can be a complicated process, with many voices being heard on any given issue. Through op-eds, analysis, breaking news, and other types of dispatches from the front lines of education reform, the media give us a window to see the process from all angles, from the opinions of students to the advice of a university dean. The media is not only actively relaying information about education and education reform, but is part of the process of reform itself as media discourse can also influence students and others as they navigate their own educational paths.

"COLLEGE COUNSELOR: HOW TO APPEAL AN ADMISSIONS DENIAL," BY RALPH BECKER, FROM THE *GRUNION GAZETTE*, APRIL 6, 2013

Receiving a rejection letter is the admissions process rite of passage. We all take our dings. Most of us duly acknowledge them, despair, and move on.

There are, however, instances where rejections might warrant an appeal—though, in all honesty, there aren't many. Schools generally do a pretty thorough job before rendering a final decision. Unless you have some new information to share with the admissions office, or there was some error (a mistake in the transcript, for example) it's unlikely the college will reconsider an application.

However, sometimes an appeals letter is necessary, even if it merely serves to put the whole process into perspective for the thwarted applicant.

Most of the highly selective schools (the Ivy League, Duke, or Stanford) will not acknowledge an appeal unless something went really askew with your application, in which case, it might be better to have your high school counselor call the admissions office and let the professionals confer (e.g. a miscalculation of GPA).

For schools that do have an appeals process (like the University of California system), appeal letters need to be written and submitted as quickly as possible. Many colleges have an April 15th appeal deadline, or earlier (UC Santa Cruz's appeal deadline was March 29th).

How do you go about writing a strong appeal letter? Foremost, be guided by common sense and maintain a positive tone. Believe in yourself and your capabilities, but also acknowledge the efforts of the admissions office.

Be pleasant. Focus on your accomplishments. Definitely do not discuss other candidates. You want the admissions office to feel badly about having rejected such a capable, articulate, nice candidate like yourself.

Before you start, carefully review the rejection letter (or online notification) to see if it mentions anything about appeals. Next, if the information isn't in the letter, go to the admissions website and research the school's appeal process. If there is a formal process, carefully follow the instructions.

Sometimes the appeal process suggests submitting an extra recommendation, if so, find a teacher and solicit one. Remember, don't resubmit the same information to the admissions office. Instead, if you recently accomplished a new meritorious activity, mention it in your appeal, and clearly explain its importance.

Appealing a decision is not for the weak willed; the Berkeley website explicitly tells you: "We strongly discourage letters of appeal unless you can provide significant new information…" so make it good. It then concludes with the ominous: "Even if you choose to appeal, we recommend that you do not delay accepting an admission offer from another college or university." In other words, they're telling you this is a long shot, and that you should have a lot of alternatives well in hand.

Don't lose heart. One student from several years ago successfully appealed his Berkeley rejection. A copy of his letter can be found online at: http://bettergrads.org/blog/2013/03/25/my-successful-letter-of-appeal-to-uc-berkeley/.

An alternative, depending on the school, is to apply for the spring semester. Another is to go elsewhere and then attempt to transfer. Hamilton College, in upstate New York, tells those it rejects which courses they should take to improve their chances should they attempt to transfer. Better still, Hamilton even waives the transfer application fee for any rejected candidate attempting to transfer within two years. Grinnell College of Iowa, one of the top liberal arts schools in the country, officially discourages appeals, but will entertain them from persuasive and articulate candidates.

Use your gut instincts in approaching appeals. You must firmly believe that you are a perfect fit for the school. This will give you the resolve to parry with the admissions office and firmly make your case. Treat it like a thwarted romance, then you'll know when to quit. Who knows, in another year, your transfer request might be found that much more appealing.

Ralph Becker, a resident of Long Beach, has been counseling students for the last 8 years. A former Yale Alumni interviewer, he holds a certificate in college counseling from UCLA Extension, and has published SAT* Vocab 800, Books A, B, C, & D.

1. When applying to transfer schools or for financial aid, such as scholarships and grants, should a student have to disclose if they were admitted after an appeal? How might this be taken positively? Negatively? Why might it be considered irrelevant?

"TURNING THE TIDE: CAN ADMISSIONS REFORMS REDEFINE ACHIEVEMENT?" BY JULIE RENEE POSSELT, FROM *THE CONVERSATION* WITH THE PARTNERSHIP OF THE UNIVERSITY OF MICHIGAN, JANUARY 27, 2016

Individualism makes America unhealthy and unequal, and college admissions offices have the power to do something about it. So argues a short but important report, Turning the Tide, released last week by the Making Caring Common (MCC) Project at the Harvard Graduate School of Education.

College admissions offices send messages to students about what society values. To change the message that individual achievement matters most, the report recommends admissions practices that balance intellectual and ethical engagement. It advises strategies for assessing community service and diversity experiences. Ultimately, it wants to redefine achievement to reduce pressure on students and improve access for low-income students.

Is this report part of a sea change in higher education?

As a professor whose research examines merit and diversity in academic gatekeeping, I think the answer to this question is a clear yes.

The question is, will their recommendations work?

The report is on the right track

For years, guidance and college counselors have prodded students to apply to colleges with the right fit, not just the best ranking. And educators have pushed to align preferences in admissions offices with higher education's public mission.

In 2003, Harvard law professor Lani Guinier proposed that admissions consider both academic and democratic merit. She argued that if colleges' mission includes preparing leaders for an increasingly diverse democracy, then admissions should reward potential for such leadership.

How to recognize and measure that leadership potential, like other so-called noncognitive factors, is still up for debate. But MCC's call to consider "authentic" experiences with diversity and "ethical engagement" fits with a more democratic notion of merit.

Around the country, educators are huddling to develop, test and refine models of holistic review that honor students' diverse strengths. Administrators and faculty are hungry for strategies that will help their student bodies reflect the country's demographic diversity.

There's a spirit of experimentation in admissions today that the strategies in Turning the Tide can support.

Here are my concerns:

I applaud MCC's initiative and support their goals in principle. However, I have at least three concerns with their recommendations:

First, it's not clear that they align with evaluation practices in admissions offices.

MCC wants to deemphasize AP courses, for example, but this won't be a powerful lever for change. The 2014 State of College Admissions report of the National Association for College Admission Counseling (NACAC) documents that since 2002, no more than 10 percent of college admissions offices treat AP/IB scores as a major factor in their decisions.

Second, the strategies it will take to enroll more low-income students in selective colleges are not the same ones needed to reduce achievement pressure.

Everyone worries about the lack of transparency in

college admissions, but concerns about pressure are largely coming out of upper-middle-class and wealthy families.

In many low-income high schools, where the real college access problem is, the concern is obtaining access to rigorous coursework and college preparation generally.

Third, even in systems that tend toward greater equity, the wealthy usually find ways to protect their privilege.

One way they do so, sociologists have shown, is by investing their resources in keeping up with the changing terms of access to high-status social institutions, including educational ones.

Participation in focused test preparation is one example, although scholars debate its benefits.

Or take my college-frenzied city of Ann Arbor: Less than three months after 80 selective colleges announced they would develop a shared online application with a digital portfolio, the city's community education provider started offering US$49 workshops titled "How to Apply to Elite Universities."

It is telling that they marketed the workshops to parents, not teens.

The fact is that "ethical engagement" could easily become the next dimension of merit through which privileged families preserve their competitive advantage.

Redefining 'good colleges'

The final recommendation of Turning the Tide – broadening students' ideas about what makes a good college – is perhaps the most important and difficult one.

Parents, employers, and graduate programs also need to take a broader view on college pedigree if they want to persuade students to do so.

Parents need to know how mixed the research record is (see here, here and here) on the link between selective college attendance and later earnings. They need to know that going to a selective college doesn't necessarily lead to greater life and job satisfaction, even if colleges market themselves that way.

Looking to how graduate programs judge what makes a good college, my own research has revealed how faculty in top-ranked graduate programs think about college affiliations when admitting Ph.D. students. I interviewed 68 professors across 10 programs and observed admissions meetings in six of them.

Faculty routinely assessed college GPA based on the perceived quality of the institution where grades had been earned. They felt this enabled them to distinguish among the many applicants with high grades.

Across the humanities, social sciences and natural sciences, professors in every program described being "impressed," "excited" and "dazzled" by affiliations with the Ivy League, as one might expect.

Beyond a belief in the superiority of their training, professors admitted being drawn into the cultural mystique surrounding elite higher education. A few noted that students from elite institutions were "presocialized" or "confident enough" for programs like their own.

One waxed eloquent about the brilliance of his own undergraduate peers at Yale, while others assumed that students who had survived the gauntlet of elite undergraduate admissions must truly be "better."

They also looked favorably on less prestigious institutions with respected undergraduate programs in their discipline. They admitted to me or revealed in committee that they had a hard time trusting applicants from unfamiliar institutions and ones with mediocre reputations.

Like the messages that parents send their children, how professors read college affiliations in graduate admissions sends messages to young people about what makes a good college.

MCC is right that updating admissions is a great strategy for cultural change. Admissions priorities subtly coerce adolescent behavior. A growing number of families organize their children's time and very lives to put them on a trajectory that (they think) will land them in college.

But to really alter the messages about achievement that students hear, change shouldn't be limited to the admissions office. Parents, employers and those of us who work in education also need to lead by example.

1. According to the author, what do the current ways we measure achievement mean for admissions?

2. What are other ways of measuring achievement that might help admissions teams fully assess possible students?

"STUDENTS DON'T NEED A 'PASSION,' THEY NEED PERSISTENCE," BY B.K. MARCUS, FROM THE FOUNDATION FOR ECONOMIC EDUCATION, MAY 4, 2016

Millennials are right to be angry about their schooling. Even the perpetrators see some of the damage they're doing.

"Escalating achievement pressure is not healthy for our youth," says Kedra Ishop, an associate vice president

for enrollment at the University of Michigan. "Young people
are suffering from higher rates of depression, anxiety, and
substance abuse as they juggle the demands of their lives,"
she told Reuters.

Ishop is one of about 80 educators who have endorsed
a Harvard University–developed proposal to reform college
admissions. Called "Turning the Tide," the plan calls for less
emphasis on test scores and more on "passion."

The good news for stressed-out college-bound
teens is that passion is easier to fake. The bad news is
that doing so can cause more long-term damage than test
anxiety or the ordeal of the application process.

THE PASSION PUSHERS

The Turning the Tide proposal emphasizes passionate involvement in social causes specifically — which
will come with its own bundle of troubles as colleges
recruit fewer bookworms and more Internet warriors —
but pushing social justice is just the latest act in higher
education's ongoing passion play.

Thirty years ago, my teenage peers and I were being
advised to pack our college applications with extracurricular activities: club memberships, "leadership roles," and
personal projects. Colleges, we were told, wanted "well-
rounded applicants." If we already had stellar grades and
solid test scores, these extracurriculars would help set us
apart from the competition, and if we showed any particular weakness in a subject or skill, the extra undertakings
might help to round out those rough edges.

Twenty-first-century teens are now being told
the opposite.

In "Top 10 Myths of College Admissions," assembled for the *Washington Post* by Steve Cohen, co-author of *The Zinch Guide to College Admissions*, Myth #1 is that colleges want well-rounded applicants.

"Sorry, no," writes Cohen. "Colleges want a kid who is devoted to — and excels at — something. The word they most often use is *passion*."

"Having a passion," explains former Princeton Review executive Dan Edmonds for *Time* magazine, "is supposed to give an applicant an edge, and every summer and fall, I see students scrambling to find and articulate their passion as they begin working on their essays."

WHAT'S PASSION GOOD FOR?

Writing for ThoughtCatalog.com, author Ryan Holiday warns, "Passion Is the Problem, Not the Solution."

I'm talking about ... unbridled enthusiasm, our willingness to pounce on what's in front of us with the full measure of our zeal, the "bundle of energy" that our teachers and bosses have assured us is our most important asset.

Every culture from the Greeks to the Christians, says Holiday, has discouraged passion. Ours seems to be the exception. What Holiday calls the *passion paradox* is "the undiscussed, destructive capacity of the trait that every book, speaker, boss and parent seems to expect from everybody."

Passion is emotional. It burns hot, and it can burn out. Perpetually passionate people move on to the next apparent passion. By itself that fervor won't foster anything sustainable. For long-term success, something very different is needed. Holiday calls it *purpose*. The example he offers illustrates yet another P-word: persistence.

Thomas Edison once explained that, in inventing, "the first step is an intuition — and comes with a burst — then difficulties arise." What set Edison apart from other inventors was tolerance for these difficulties, his willingness to tackle the kinds of problems that are endemic to the process — not exceptions to it — and the steady dedication with which he applied himself towards solving them.

Edison is a good choice to illustrate this distinction. At a press conference in 1929, the inventor famously said, "What it boils down to is 1 percent inspiration and 99 percent perspiration."

If there is a productive form of passion, it is not the inspiring kind. It is the slow-burning sort that sustains an Edison through the arduous 99 percent of the process. Maybe Edison had passion, but Holiday's *purpose* seems better suited to describe whatever it is that fuels that level of persistence.

PASSION'S PERILS

"Purpose" and "persistence" are not the words that admissions departments emphasize, however.

In "Our Push for 'Passion,' and Why It Harms Kids," parenting author Lisa Heffernan writes, "By the time a child rounds the corner into high school ... the conventional wisdom is that he needs to have a passion that is deep, easy to articulate, well documented and makes him stand out from the crowd."

That's great news for those who already do have a deep and well-documented drive, but "when children can't find their elusive passions, yet feel compelled to proclaim one, they grab onto an interest, label it a passion and buy the requisite instrument or equipment." This wouldn't be a problem "if passion were just a matter of semantics, a word heedlessly thrown around in place of interest or pastime.... But seeking a passion in childhood or adolescence has become an obsession in itself, and it is not without costs."

"Fake passions" she warns, "crowd out real ones."

THE PASSION GLUT

Notice that Hefferman employs economic concepts such as *hidden costs* and *crowding out.* She's right to imply that the passion surplus is an economic phenomenon, but she could have taken her analysis further. While she recognizes that the "parental obsession with passion is encouraged by the college admissions process," she does not discuss the purse strings behind that process.

We're so used to the current state of higher education that we take it as natural, rarely questioning the forces that have shaped the education industry and the preparations required for matriculation. But if you think of the university system's product as learning, or its service as teaching, then it should seem puzzling that the customers have to jump through so many hoops to acquire the goods they want.

Where else do we see would-be buyers having to compete in so many not-directly-financial ways to acquire the goods or services they seek? City housing? Socialized medicine? Employment? In each case, government interventions keep prices inflexible, supply limited, or demand artificially stimulated.

In the market for education, supply is constricted by the cartelizing process of accreditation; demand is exaggerated through tax-subsidized tuitions and a government-managed financial-aid and student-loan system. As a result, there are too many students chasing too few institutions, and while tuitions may be rising, the money price of a university education cannot play the same role as prices do in less hampered markets: it cannot attract new competition on the supply side of schooling, which would then bring down those prices; it is not yet causing enough customers to seek substitutes, thereby putting pressure on suppliers to offer real alternatives that may better fit students' differing needs. Instead, universities offer a standardized product, and admissions offices require applicants to compete in ever more nonmonetary ways.

When too many applicants had good grades, we had to start competing on our well-roundedness. Once everyone filled their applications with extracurriculars, admissions offices had to find some other criterion for selecting the few from the many. If the passion glut continues, we should expect to see either new criteria or newly specific variations on the old ones: that is why admissions departments are about to replace the push for passion in general with a more precise passion for social activism.

Complicating the economics of education even further is confusion on what exactly counts as the product.

SIGNAL TO NOISE

In "Yes, Students Are Customers, but..." economist Steve Horwitz and special education teacher Kevin Currie-Knight suggest that one problem with modern education is that buyers and sellers don't agree on what is being bought or sold. Producers may think they're selling knowledge and skills, while consumers believe they are buying the diploma, a signal to future employers that a graduate is worth hiring.

Brian Caplan, author of the forthcoming book *The Case Against Education*, believes that 30–80 percent of the value of a liberal arts education is in precisely such "signaling," rather than the intrinsic value of what students study or teachers teach. The irony of the college application process, then, is that applicants are generating fake passions as an empty signal of their worthiness to an institution that will provide not skills or training so much as yet more signals to some other institution later in the student's life.

As we pursue the signaling value of more and more passion, we achieve less and less substance. It's not just that the passion signaling is empty; it's that premature passions discourage the mature variety, the kind that looks more like purpose. While we're trying to burn hot for the pursuit we've convinced ourselves we're the most passionate about, we're doing less experimenting and are therefore less likely to find the right fit. It's like marrying the first classmate you kissed and missing out on the deeper adult relationship you would otherwise have found later. Some know their true love before they're 20, but most of us need more time. A government cartelized and subsidized industry telling us to settle down as soon as possible is a formula for waste and heartbreak.

Will an ongoing surfeit of pseudo-passion produce a new lost generation, a population of searchers unable to settle deeply into the interests or jobs or relationships that require patience, persistence, and a sense of thoughtful openness? Today's teens may prove more resilient than that, at least in the long run. But in the short term, there's a rude awakening for those who are fooled by the admissions process. Passion may get you into college, but it won't get you through it. Passion might get you a job, but it won't help you succeed in it.

The alternative is not a return to the well-rounded applicant or the straight-A student. It's a system without any central plan or government funding, where both the supply of and demand for learning are left to find their own balance. Until that happens, young millennials may need to withdraw their consent individually, step off the passion treadmill, and seek educational options that do less damage.

1. What role does passion play in what schools students are applying to? Is that a good thing, or is it dangerous?

2. What does the author think is the most important factor in a student's education? Why?

CHAPTER 6

WHAT AVERAGE PEOPLE SAY

There are many stakeholders in the debate on higher education and college admissions, but few are more invested than the average citizens trying to navigate the process themselves. Students and the parents or guardians who help guide them enter into a complex—and often mysterious—process that can have a significant impact on their lives. Just as invested are the admissions teams and others who are receiving stacks of applications and trying to sort through who is the strongest potential student. Their voices are equally important to experts and others, and provide us with an understanding of the needs, achievements, and concerns that will decide the future of college admissions.

"THE REAL CAUSE OF CAMPUS RACISM," BY JAMES HUFFMAN, FROM THE HOOVER INSTITUTION, DECEMBER 15, 2015

Like the 1812 earthquake that rumbled from its epicenter at New Madrid, Missouri, to New England, Georgia and other distant locations, this fall's protests at the University of Missouri spread to colleges in every corner of the country.

At Harvard, a group of law students launched a campaign to remove the school's seal because it contains the coat of arms of a slave owner. At Dartmouth, students and faculty marched in solidarity with black students at the University of Missouri in what was called a "black out" (the marchers all wore black). After days of protests at Yale, the university president announced plans for more academic study of race and ethnicity and for improvements in the experiences of people of color. At Princeton a debate inspired by objections to the university's use of the name of former university president (and president of the United States) Woodrow Wilson is ongoing. Everywhere, university administrators are scrambling to assure their students of color that their schools really do care.

In response to the continuing protests, much has been written and spoken about how universities can best serve the interests of their students of color. Those who sympathize with the protesters argue that students of color, in particular, should be nurtured and protected from uncomfortable experiences that distract from their education. Others insist that true education depends on students experiencing discomfort so they are better prepared to cope with the discomforts they will inevitably face in the future. No doubt there are good points to be considered on both sides of the question. Every campus has its boors and jerks whose bad behaviors might warrant chastisement from university officials, although peer disapproval is almost always a more effective remedy.

Whether and when offensive speech should be prohibited are more difficult questions. The boundary between gratuitous verbal assault and the free expression essential to the academy is not always easily drawn, although a few institutions have followed the example of the University of Chicago in making clear that their default position is free speech.

Sadly, Americans seem to lose any capacity for reasoned discussion when alleged personal assaults are said to stem from racial animus. Disagreements deteriorate into verbal and often physical violence, with an almost conclusive presumption of racism whenever racism is alleged. In this climate, college administrators see only two options. They can resign, as did the University of Missouri president and the dean of students at Claremont McKenna (after writing an email to which students of color took offense). Or they can accede to protesters' demands for safe spaces, sensitivity training, trigger warnings, expanded diversity offices, and rapid response to allegations of discrimination and hurt.

But there is a third way. Colleges and universities should examine how their own policies and programs encourage racial division.

At the time of the University of Missouri protests, a story in the *New York Times* reported that students of color at the university felt isolated and disrespected. They, particularly the black students, tend to hang out together. According to a student quoted in the Times story, an area in the student center where blacks sit is called "the black hole." There is little real integration, say both white and black students. Visit the cafeteria of almost any campus with even a small population of black students and you will see the equivalent of the University of Missouri's black hole.

Do students of color hang out together because they feel disrespected and discriminated against—because they are excluded? Or is it a matter of choice rooted in racial pride, perceived cultural difference, and a desire to preserve and protect that difference from the dominant white culture? While the protesters would surely assert their right to racial self-segregation for reasons of pride, solidarity and culture, they do not hesitate to claim that disrespect and discrimination by other students and school officials prevent their full and equal participation in the university. To be clear, no one is claiming that students of color are being denied access to higher education—the sort of discrimination James Meredith experienced a half century ago at the University of Mississippi. Rather, today's discrimination is said to take the form of "micro-aggressions"—subtle actions and loaded language that slowly eat away at self-confidence and the sense of belonging.

Are colleges and universities responsible for the isolation and exclusion the protesters claim to experience, and for the de facto segregation that exists on most campuses? In significant ways they are, but not, for the most part, for the reasons said to justify the protests at the University of Missouri and elsewhere. There is little campus administrators can do, beyond declarations of disapproval, to prevent offensive comments, or even explicitly racist statements and actions of usually anonymous individuals. If the past two decades of sensitivity training haven't solved that problem, there is little reason to think more of the same will help.

The core of the problem is that the vast majority of our colleges and universities have made race and racial differences central to almost everything they do. And to make matters worse, those who accredit our universities make attention to race in admissions and programming a condition of accreditation.

Central to the mission of the University of Missouri is diversity, described on the school's website as "not an end to itself" but "a means for students, faculty and staff to experience firsthand the increasing multicultural world that we live in." And what are the means for achieving diversity and the measure of success? The means is the admissions process and the measure of success is the degree to which the races of those admitted reflect the racial makeup of the state and nation. Whatever the university may claim to the contrary, race is a key factor in admissions, as it is at almost every other college and university in the country.

Once the racially balanced student body arrives at the University of Missouri, minority students have a wide array of options provided especially for them. For example, black students can enroll in black studies with a minor in multicultural studies. They can apply for many different "diversity-related scholarships." They can join one of seven "historically black fraternities or sororities." They can hang out at the Black Culture Center and join the African Students Association, the Mizzou Black Men's Initiative, the Mizzou Black Women's Initiative, the Association of Black Graduate and Professional Students, the Legion of Black Collegians, the

Black Business Students Association and the Black Law Students Association, just to name a few. Meanwhile their fellow white students can enroll in any number of diversity and sensitivity training courses all under the watchful eye of the vice-chancellor for inclusion.

Can there be any surprise that students of color feel as if they are treated differently from white students when their admission to the university is very likely to have been influenced by their race? When they, and only they, are often invited to campus a week early, purportedly to bond with their fellow students of color and to give them a head start on college? When one of their first experiences on campus is some sort of gathering with other students of color? When they are directed to the campus office of diversity or minority affairs as a place for counseling? When they are invited to join the Black or Hispanic or Pacific Islander or Native Hawaiian student union? When they learn they can major in Black, etc. studies?

No factor, not even athletic prowess, is more significant to college admissions than race. Diversity is a core mission for the vast majority of institutions and students of color know that means them. Students of color know themselves to be what we now call, in a terrible corruption of the language, "diverse" individuals. Special programming for minority students cannot help but convey, in a micro-aggression-like manner, that campus officials believe students of color need extra help to succeed. School sanctioned programs and groups that cater to students of color, even students of particular colors, segregate students on the basis of race. Separate minority counseling services reinforce the idea that students of color are different, that counselors of a different race cannot possibly understand a minority student's issues and concerns. Some universities even provide separate (dare one say segregated) housing for students of particular races.

All of this focus on race cannot help but influence the thinking of white students. Even before going to college, most white students have been taught in secondary and even primary school that minority kids are different and that as white students they need to be sensitive to those differences. When they apply to colleges, white students know that they have a disadvantage in the admissions process. Once they arrive on campus, they witness university-sponsored and endorsed programming directed at students of color. Now they are learning that they need to shelve their "white privilege," notwithstanding that many of their minority classmates may have come from economic or family circumstances far better than theirs.

Whatever privilege students may have before they arrive at college, the reality of American higher education today is that students of color have been privileged by their institutions in ways that invite segregation and differential treatment, whether done in the name of reparations for past discrimination, as affirmative action to overcome societally imposed disadvantages, or in the belief that celebrating and encouraging differences improves education for everyone. There should be no surprise that students of color often self-segregate and are seen as different by their fellow students.

The concept of white privilege is a logical outgrowth of the concept of institutional racism. In reaction to the now quaint notion that intent to discriminate must be proven to establish illegal race discrimination, lawyers and race scholars came up with the concept of institutional racism. The idea is that racism is so deeply rooted in American society that it persists even amongst institutions that have made genuine efforts to correct for any intentional past discrimination. Thus, the theory holds, the University of Missouri and all of its privileged white students are guilty, by definition, of racial discrimination today, albeit in subtle ways.

But there is nothing subtle about the most pervasive form of racial discrimination prevailing at most American colleges and universities today. It is done in the name of lifting up those who have been discriminated against in the past. But there should be little wonder that the intended beneficiaries of this allegedly benign discrimination feel themselves isolated and treated differently. By design, universities have isolated them and treated them differently.

1. What do you think about the author's argument here? Is it problematic in any way?

2. How might these racial policies at universities influence the admissions process as well?

"ADMISSIONS DIRECTORS AT PUBLIC UNIVERSITIES SPEAK HONESTLY (AND ANONYMOUSLY) ABOUT THEIR GOALS," BY MARIAN WANG, FROM PROPUBLICA, SEPTEMBER 18, 2013

As we detailed last week, many public universities, suffering from state budget cuts or hungry for prestige, have made it a priority to attract out-of-state students, who pay higher tuition, and those who will help boost the schools' place in college rankings.

But a newly released survey by Inside Higher Ed of admissions directors directly about their priorities, allowing them to respond anonymously. The survey, of course, is of admissions directors -- so it's focused more on what type of students schools are going after in the recruitment stage, and less on the students who gets financial aid as a sweetener to prompt enrollment.

Still, it's a reflection of some of the same priorities -- including a strong interest in out-of-state students and international students, who typically bring in more revenue, even with modest discounts.

For instance, 80 percent of admissions directors surveyed at public four-year universities agreed or strongly agreed that they were likely to increase their efforts to recruit out-of-state students. The percentage was slightly lower -- but still 66 percent to 72 percent, depending on the type of public institution -- for international students.

The survey also has some telling results about the popularity of so-called merit aid, which universities use to give discounts to particularly appealing students.

About two-thirds of admissions directors at public universities said that they would likely increase their efforts to recruit students with merit scholarships. Most also said they didn't see a problem with using institutional resources on merit aid -- even though as we noted, investing resources in merit aid often means giving it to students who don't need it, and not having much left over for those who do.

Over the long term, state schools have been giving a growing share of their grants to wealthier students, and a declining share to the poorest students, as we reported.

They've also been serving a shrinking portion of the nation's needy students, leaving community colleges and for-profit colleges to take on more of that responsibility.

Asked about first-generation college students, the responses from admissions directors indicated that they were also a target population, though perhaps less so relative to out-of-state or international populations: 62 percent of admissions directors at public research universities said they'd likely increase recruitment efforts for first-generation populations, and that figure was 55 percent for master's/bachelor's degree public institutions.

1. Why might school admissions directors want to be anonymous when speaking about the admissions process?

2. What does this survey tell you about what admissions teams look for in candidates?

"RECRUITER'S EXPERIENCE AT ONE FOR-PROFIT UNIVERSITY SUGGESTS REFORM EFFORTS WILL FACE HURDLES," BY SHARONA COUTTS, FROM *PROPUBLICA*, FEBRUARY 14, 2011

When Ryan Richardson took a job as a recruiter at Grand Canyon University last summer, he was no novice to the business of for-profit colleges.

He had worked as an enrollment counselor at the University of Phoenix, the biggest school in the sector, for years before leaving to pursue his dream of playing professional baseball.

Richardson had heard that Grand Canyon was a good place to work: that it treated employees well and that—as a Christian university—it did not use the high-pressure sales tactics that had made him uncomfortable working at the University of Phoenix. But within days of starting at the school, Richardson said, he had a growing sense of disillusionment at the techniques the university was using to recruit students.

"I remember calling my Dad and telling him it was just like the University of Phoenix, except they'd implemented God into the mix," Richardson said.

Richardson says he became so dismayed that he decided to record meetings, training sessions and conversations with Grand Canyon managers and other staff during the four months he stayed on the job, ending when he quit last October. The recordings, as well as other documents and internal e-mails that Richardson provided to ProPublica, give an unflattering inside view of how one team of recruiters at the school was seeking to bring in students.

For-profit schools' recruitment methods have been the subject of intense scrutiny over the last year, as government investigators, lawmakers and regulators have taken aim at tactics deemed abusive or deceptive. Last week, Sen. Tom Harkin, D-Iowa, chairman of the Senate Committee on Health, Education, Labor and Pensions, decried for-profit schools' "systemic effort to enroll students at any costs."

New federal measures to rein in certain recruitment practices are scheduled to take effect this summer.
Richardson's experience suggests it may be difficult for
some schools to change their long-standing sales culture.

With just over 42,000 students and a market
capitalization of around $800 million, Phoenix-based
Grand Canyon is one of the smaller publicly traded
for-profit schools, some of which have burgeoned into
multi-billion dollar enterprises.

The University of Phoenix has around
438,000 students and net revenues of nearly $4.5 billion
last year, according to regulatory filings. Kaplan Higher
Education, which is owned by the *Washington Post*
Company, has over 100,000 students, and DeVry Inc., which
owns DeVry University, had about 130,000, according to
company spokespeople.

Grand Canyon has relatively low loan default rates,
according to recently released government data and was
not named in a recent Government Accountability Office
report that found fraudulent recruiting practices at 15
other for-profit colleges.

Richardson started at the school last June. He had
just been released by the St. Paul Saints, a Minnesota
team unaffiliated with Major League Baseball, after a
quixotic attempt to revive his aspirations to be a catcher,
at age 27.

He said he was drawn to Grand Canyon because
he believed the company's chief executive, Brian Mueller,
operated an ethical for-profit college. Mueller took
over Grand Canyon after more than two decades at the
University of Phoenix and its parent company, the
Apollo Group, including a stint as company president.

Almost immediately, however, Richardson said he was taken aback by the way his manager, Isabel Ford, a long-time Grand Canyon employee, prodded her 12-member team to call prospective recruits as many as four times a day and coached him to be more aggressive in signing up students.

"You have to ride the bull a little bit harder," Ford can be heard telling Richardson in a recording he provided.

Richardson refused to pressure people into enrolling in the doctoral program, he said. Instead, he insisted on giving candidates all the information he thought they needed before signing up. He said he never tried to dissuade anyone from attending Grand Canyon, but they simply chose to go elsewhere or stopped answering his calls.

Grand Canyon confirmed that Richardson resigned without notice.

Ford sent e-mails instructing Richardson to make 100 calls and leave 100 messages per day. He also was given so-called "blitz lists," names and numbers to blast with multiple calls throughout a given day.

Some of the people he was directed to call repeatedly were not interested in signing up for Grand Canyon, Richardson said. In a recording he provided to ProPublica, a woman pleaded with him to stop calling, saying the school had the wrong number and that she had been receiving calls from multiple recruiters each day.

Among the training materials provided to Richardson was a document titled "Creating Urgency-Guidelines," with topic headings that included, "Set the Pace," "Focus on the Finish," and "Don't Stop at No." Ford listened in on Richardson's recruitment calls, instructing him on how he could capitalize on prospective students' emotional cues to persuade them to sign up.

"I would have said, 'What is it that you were hoping to get out of a doctoral degree?' " Ford said, reviewing Richardson's pitch to a woman on the school's doctoral program in education. "Right then, you would have known the vanity thing, because that came out. She just wants 'doctor.' "

In his speech on Monday, Harkin criticized for-profit schools for manipulating potential applicants' emotions in order to get them to sign up. He pointed to ITT Technical Institute, Kaplan University, and Corinthian Colleges, where documents or staff statements have shown that recruiters were taught to identify prospects' "pain" as a lever to prompt them to enroll.

Ford still works at Grand Canyon, but she declined to comment when reached at work.

In an interview last month, Mueller called Ford's conduct "inappropriate" and "disappointing" and said she had been "counseled." He said the documents given to Richardson were not official company training materials.

Grand Canyon allowed ProPublica to review its training materials, which explained federal laws on telemarketing and gave detailed instructions on how to make recruitment calls. One sheet said that, following a recruiter's call, "The potential student should walk away feeling educated and knowledgeable, ready to make the best decision for him/herself."

But a lawsuit filed in 2007 asserts that Grand Canyon had relied on high-pressure recruiting tactics. The complaint describes a meeting of top executives, during which the director of ground enrollment said recruiters were participating in contests to boost the number of new students at the college of education. The suit also cites an e-mail from the director of business development and enrollment that says recruiters who signed up 25 new students would receive a $25 gift card.

According to the complaint, the company took top-performing recruiters to an annual ski vacation in Lake Tahoe. The company settled the suit for $5.2 million last August but did not admit liability.

Richardson said recruiters were not rewarded for signing up students, but they knew their jobs were on the line if they did not. He said they were also rewarded in more subtle ways that nevertheless encouraged them to pressure people to enroll.

For instance, a training document called "Retention Strategies" refers to bonuses that recruiters could earn when students they enrolled had completed a certain number of course credits.

"Remember that it is not just a Reg[istration], it's an enrollment that pays off in the future if you take care of it," the presentation says. "The more you invest, the more you will get in return."

Richardson said he obtained the PowerPoint presentation from a computer drive that was accessible to all staff members.

Mueller would not give details on the amount of such bonuses, saying the information was proprietary, but admissions experts and regulators said incentives linked to signing up students could be corrosive.

"We believe this practice contains significant potential for abuse," said James Kvaal, deputy undersecretary for Education.

Under the federal rules that take effect in July, such bonuses will no longer be permitted. Mueller said Grand Canyon would phase them out in order to comply.

The new regulations target misleading or overly aggressive recruiting practices by restoring a ban on tying recruiters' pay to the number of new students they enroll and strengthen the Department of Education's ability to take action against deceptive marketing.

To discourage schools from pressuring people to sign up for courses in which they are unlikely to succeed, the regulations also link colleges' eligibility to participate in federal student aid programs to the ability of their students to repay loans, Education Department spokesman Justin Hamilton said.

The draft of the rule elicited tens of thousands of public comments and was the focus of an intense public relations and lobbying drive by both supporters and opponents. The department delayed the full finalization of the rule but expects to publish the entire text early this year, Hamilton said.

A spokesman for the University of Phoenix said the school has already implemented changes to its enrollment procedures, including "completely eliminating enrollment results as a component of enrollment advisor compensation."

Harkin has said he plans to introduce legislation aimed at abuses in the for-profit sector, and his committee is planning more hearings into proprietary schools.

Richardson, who now works at a data processing company, said he never enrolled a single student at Grand Canyon. He quit in late October, when he says he could no longer stomach the pressure to sign people up. Yet he doesn't think he was a bad enrollment counselor.

"If I could have found someone who was genuinely going to benefit from the program, then I would have registered them," he said.

1. How do for-profit schools differ from non-profit schools? How does this impact admissions?

2. Why does Richardson think reforming these institutions will be difficult? What are some steps that could be taken?

"A DEAN'S PLEA: LET STUDENTS DISCOVER KNOWLEDGE WITHOUT PRESSURE TO IMPRESS," BY JOANN MCKENNA, FROM *THE CONVERSATION*, APRIL 29, 2015

Is today's competitive environment making high school students pursue a polished resume and not their passion?

As a university vice president and an admissions dean, we've just finished contacting students whom we did admit, did not admit and would have liked to admit, but simply couldn't.

Regardless of outcome, each group had in its midst students who have been caught up in the growing phenomenon of credentialism, a practice of relying on formal qualifications, that too often undermines what should be four wonderful years of self-discovery in high school.

MORE THAN A NUMBERS GAME

Whether it's taking an Advance Placement course that really doesn't interest them, holding office in an organization because it will "look good," on their resume or playing a sport that they really don't enjoy, students are too often trying to impress, instead of trying to discover, enjoy and grow.

Every student seeking admission to college wants to present a "strong case."

But what's becoming increasingly clear to admission officers like me and to guidance counselors who advise high school students, is that "credentialism" is being practiced more and more by students, high schools and institutions of higher learning.

To some degree we have ourselves to blame.

College rankings rely heavily on metrics and lets face it, people love being on the "A" list. In some cases, the metrics are about the school; in others, about the students who apply and are admitted.

We begin, despite our best intentions, to question not whether a student is a good match for our institution but how admitting the student will affect our "profile."

Too often I worry that colleges feel obligated to play the "numbers" game and admit students solely on the basis of board scores, grade scores, number of AP courses, number of extracurricular activities, number of recommendations and so on.

STUDENTS ARE NOT PURSUING THEIR PASSION

As a result, many students – urged on by their parents, teachers, guidance counselors, and, yes, colleges and universities – conduct their lives as though the only purpose is to build a resume to get into the "best" school they can.

So what's wrong with that?

For colleges and universities, that means we assess

students on professed interest and performance that don't always reflect what the student is really all about and capable of doing. And that's not good for the student or the institution.

It subverts our desire not just to recruit and admit a class but to create a class, one whose members will thrive synergistically, often energized more by their differences than by their similarities.

For students, it turns their high school careers into a grab bag of experiences, many of which were pursued to impress others rather than for self-discovery and the pursuit of interests and excellence for their own sake.

Don't get me wrong.

Many students are truly driven by the best motivations to understand their interests, abilities, and aspirations.

But too many are told they need to go to the right schools, study the right courses, participate in the right activities, have the right friends, volunteer for the right programs, plan for the right careers...and on and on.

What often results is an early and unwelcome appreciation for Thoreau's observation that, "The mass of men lead lives of quiet desperation."

Too many students fail to understand that they are quintessentially "a work in progress," always in the process of becoming, never finished. (Most adults aren't much different.)

And in our rush to help them prepare for the rest of their lives, we prevent them from taking full advantage of what's going on right now in their lives.

Students deserve better, from everybody who is pressuring them to display success to impress rather than for its inherent self-worth.

COLLEGES NEED TO RESTORE LOVE FOR LEARNING

Can colleges and universities help?

We can proclaim that we seek more than numbers, more than honors, more than achievement for its promotional value. And we can demonstrate our commitment by accepting students whose accomplishments are rooted in exploration, passion, self-discovery and even plain old fun.

We tell students that college is a launching pad for successful careers and lives. And that's what it should be.

Both high schools and colleges may do students a grave disservice if we suggest that resume-building trumps exploration in pursuit of self-awareness and fulfillment.

So what should we be telling our young people as they undertake their journey to what we pray will be successful lives and careers?

Here are some things that I suggest to help guide that journey:

- Establish what really matters to you so you'll have a compass.
- Invest in yourself. You have gifts that need to be developed.
- Do the best with what you have. It's OK if you aren't good at some things.
- Take risks. But be smart about it.
- Own it – it's your life. Take responsibility for it.
- Build integrity; above all else, this is what matters.
- Find mentors who inspire you.

This isn't meant to be a "feel good" list.

And it isn't just a list meant for the students. We must remain committed to a holistic evaluation.

As educators, we need to restore equity, perspective and a reverence for excellence for its own sake.

We need to connect our kids with the wisdom — from family, friends and trusted institutions — that previously helped each generation blossom, for their individual and collective benefit.

If we can't come together to change the system, then shame on us.

1. What do students lose when they are unable to enjoy education, as the author argues?

2. How can administrators make sure students are not overly concerned about getting into college and can focus on learning?

"WHY 1904 TESTING METHODS SHOULD NOT BE USED FOR TODAY'S STUDENTS," BY ROBERT STERNBER, FROM *THE CONVERSATION*, NOVEMBER 18, 2015

When I was an elementary school student, schools in my hometown administered IQ tests every couple of years. I felt very scared of the psychologist who came in to give those tests.

I also performed terribly. As a result, at one point, I was moved to a lower-grade classroom so I could take a test more suitable to my IQ level.

Consequently, I believed that my teachers considered me stupid. I, of course, thought I was stupid. In addition, I also thought my teachers expected low-quality work from a child of such low IQ. So, I gave them what they expected.

Had it not been for my fourth grade teacher, who thought there was more to a person than an IQ test score, I almost certainly would not be a professor today.

You might think things have gotten better. Not quite. I have two generations of children (from different marriages), and something similar happened to both my sons: Seth, age 36, now a successful entrepreneur in Silicon Valley, and Sammy, age four.

Some children as young as Sammy take preschool tests. And almost all our students – at least those wanting to go on to college – take what one might call proxies for IQ tests – the SAT and ACT – which are IQ tests by another name.

Testing is compromising the future of many of our able students. Today's testing comes at the expense of validity (strong prediction of future success), equity (ensuring that members of various groups have an equal shot), and common sense in identifying those students who think deeply and reflectively rather than those who are good at answering shallow multiple-choice questions.

How should today's students be assessed?

INTELLIGENCE TESTS IN HALLOWEEN COSTUMES

Psychology professor Douglas Detterman and his colleagues have shown that the SAT and the ACT are little more than disguised IQ tests.

They may look slightly different from the IQ tests, but they closely resemble the intelligence tests used by Charles

Spearman (1904), Alfred Binet and Theodore Simon (1916), famous psychologists in Great Britain and France, respectively, who created the first IQ tests a century ago.

While these tests may have been at the cutting edge at the turn of the 20th century, today they are archaic. Imagine using medical tests designed at the beginning of the 20th century to diagnose, say, cancer or heart disease.

People's success today scarcely hinges on solving simple, pat academic problems with unique solutions conveniently presented as multiple-choice options.

When your kids (or colleagues) misbehave, does anyone give you five options, one of which is uniquely correct, to solve the problem of how to get them to behave properly?

Or, are there any multiple-choice answers for how to solve serious crises, whether in international affairs (eg, in Syria), in business (eg, at Volkswagen) or in education (eg, skyrocketing college tuitions)?

HOW DO WE TEST FOR SUCCESS?

The odd thing is that we can do much better. That would mean taking into account that academic and life success involves much more than IQ.

In my research conducted with my colleagues who include Florida State University professor Richard Wagner and a former professor at the US Military Academy at West Point, George Forsythe, we found that success in managerial, military and other leadership jobs can be predicted independent of IQ levels.

More generally, we have found that practical intelligence, or common sense, is itself largely independent of IQ.

Moreover, my research with Todd Lubart, now a professor at the University of Paris V, has shown that creative intelligence also is distinct from IQ.

My colleagues and I, including Professor Elena Grigorenko at Yale, have shown in studies on five continents that children from diverse cultures, such as Yup'ik Eskimos in Alaska, Latino-American students in San Jose, California, and rural Kenyan schoolchildren, may have practical adaptive skills that far exceed those of their teachers (such as how to hunt in the frozen tundra, ice-fish, or treat parasitic illnesses such as malaria with natural herbal medicines).

Yet teachers – and IQ tests – may view these children as intellectually challenged.

WHAT ARE WE TESTING, ANYWAY?

Our theory of "successful intelligence" can help predict the academic, extracurricular and leadership success of college students. In addition, it could increase applications from qualified applicants and decrease differences among ethnic groups, such as between African-American and Euro-American students, that are found in the SAT/ACT.

The idea behind "successful intelligence" is not only to measure analytical skills as is done by the SAT/ACT, but also other skills that are important to college and life success. Although this does mean additional testing, it is an assessment of strength-based skills that actually are fun to take.

What are these other skills and assessments, exactly?

The truth is, you can't get by in life only on analytical skills – you also need to come up with your own new ideas (creativity), know how to apply your ideas (practical common sense), and ensure they benefit others beside yourself (wisdom).

So, assessments of "successful intelligence" would measure creativity, common sense and wisdom/ethics, in addition to analytical skills, as measured by the SAT/ACT.

Here is how measurement of successful intelligence works:

Creative skills can be measured by having students write or tell a creative story, design a scientific experiment, draw something new, caption a cartoon or suggest what the world might be like today if some past event (such as the defeat of the Nazis in World War II) had turned out differently.

Practical skills can be measured by having students watch several videos of college students facing practical problems — and then solving the problems for the students in the videos, or by having students comment on how they persuaded a friend of some ideas that the friend did not initially accept.

Wisdom-based and ethical skills can be measured by problems such as what to do upon observing a student cheating, or commenting on how one could, in the future, make a positive and meaningful difference to the world, at some level.

A NEW WAY TO TEST

My collaborators and I first tested our ideas between 2000 and 2005 when I was IBM professor of psychology and education and professor of management at Yale. We found (in our "Rainbow Project") that we could double prediction of freshman-year grades over that obtained from the SAT.

Also, relative to the SAT, we reduced by more than half ethnic-group differences between Euro-Americans, Asian-Americans, African-Americans, Latino-Americans and American Indians.

Later in 2011, I engaged, in collaboration with Lee Coffin, dean of undergraduate admissions at Tufts University, in a project called Kaleidoscope. At the time, I was dean of arts and sciences at Tufts. Kaleidoscope was optional for all undergraduate applicants to Tufts – tens of thousands did Kaleidoscope over the years.

We increased prediction not only of academic success, but also of extracurricular and leadership success, while greatly reducing ethnic-group differences.

Then again, when I was provost and senior vice president of Oklahoma State University (OSU), in collaboration with Kyle Wray, VP for enrollment management, we implemented a similar program at OSU (called the "Panorama Project") that also was available to all applicants.

The measures are still being used at Tufts and at Oklahoma State. These projects have resulted in students being admitted to Tufts and OSU who never would have made it on the basis of the high school GPAs and SATs.

On our assessments, the students displayed potential that was hidden by traditional standardized tests and even by high school grades.

THE PROBLEM OF BEING STUCK

So why don't colleges move on?

There are several reasons, but the most potent is sheer inertia and fear of change.

College and university presidents and admissions

deans around the country have revealed to me in informal conversations that they want change but are afraid to rock the boat.

Moreover, because the SAT, unlike our assessment, is highly correlated with socioeconomic status, colleges like it. College tuition brings in big money, and anything that could affect the dollars is viewed with fear. Students who do well on standardized tests are more likely to be full-pay students, an attraction to institutions of higher learning.

As I know only too well, colleges mostly do what they did before, and changes often require approval of many different stakeholders. The effort to effect change can be daunting.

Finally, there is the problem of self-fulfilling prophecy. We use conventional standardized tests to select students. We then give those high-scoring students better opportunities not only in college but for jobs in our society.

As a result, the tests often make their predictions come true. Given my family history, I know all too well how real the problem of self-fulfilling prophecies is.

1. What role does testing play in college admissions? What can testing show admissions teams, and what can't it show?

2. What are other ways to measure student potential and performance?

CONCLUSION

College admissions are an exciting, nerve-wracking process for students across the country and around the world. The process is also complicated for those making the selections from a wide pool of talented applicants, all bringing something new and different to the schools to which they apply. Higher education is an important source of opportunity and growth, and can guide the future of our country. But it has also been the focus of numerous debates surrounding race, income inequality, gender discrimination, and other important questions that face society.

Although none of those questions have easy answers, as we've seen in this book the debates surrounding them are lively and vigorous, and have implications for everyday Americans and international students. The way we approach education and who has access to it determines the way our country is able to grow, respond to changes in evolving fields, and contribute to areas from the arts to the sciences.

In this book, we've had a close-up investigation of the admissions process, from the perspective of low-income students trying to get into elite schools, admissions directors trying to reform the way they do their job, and experts examining the large-scale impact admissions have on issues beyond the classroom. We've seen how the courts interpret rights in the context of admissions and how politicians view educational policy. We've also learned how factors like race, income, and gender can impact admissions decisions, what is being done to ensure biases have no place in the admissions process, and how all students can capitalize on their potential at schools that will challenge them and help them grow. College admissions is just one step on the long road to the future for many students, but it is an important one that is constantly changing, evolving, and reshaping how we engage with education.

BIBLIOGRAPHY

Becker, Ralph. "College Counselor: How To Appeal An Admissions Denial." *Grunion Gazette*, April 6, 2013. http://www .gazettes.com/news/education/college-counselor-how-to-ap peal-an-admissions-denial/article_4debaa10-9d7b-11e2-8cdf -001a4bcf887a.html.

Brown, Claire. "Ideas From Abroad: Reforming the Australian University Admissions System." *The Conversation*, August 15, 2016. https://theconversation.com/ideas-from-abroad-reform ing-the-australian-university-admissions-system-63873.

Bustos, Cheri et al. "Letter to the Honorable Bruce Rauner, Governor of Illinois." *US Congressman Rodney Davis*, April 11, 2016. http://rodneydavis.house.gov/news/documentsingle.aspx? DocumentID=399044.

Coutts, Sharona. "Recruiter's Experience at one For-Profit University Suggests Reform Efforts Will Face Hurdles." *ProPublica*, February 14, 2011. https://www.propublica.org/article/recruit ers-experience-at-one-for-profit-university-suggests-reform -efforts.

Delwiche, Theodore R. "Suite Alleges Race-Based Discrimination in Harvard Admissions Practices." *Harvard Crimson*, November 18, 2014. http://www.thecrimson.com /article/2014/11/18/law-suit-admissions-alleged-discrimination.

Foster, Bill et al. "Letter ot the Honorable Bruce Rauner, Governor of Illinois." *US House of Representatives*, April 11, 2016. https://foster.house.gov/sites/foster.house.gov /files/2016.04.11_SENT_Ltr.%20to%20Gov.%20Illinois%20 Higher%20Education.pdf.

Garces, Liliana M. and Gary Orfield. "Explainer: Crucial Texas Case on Race Considerations in College Admissions." *The Conversation*, July 2, 2015. https://theconversation.com /explainer-crucial-texas-case-on-race-considerations-in -college-admissions-44117.

Hands, Africa S. "Handling Objections," from *Successfully Serving the College Bound* (Chicago, IL: American Library Association, 2014).

Hannah-Jones, Nikole. "What Abigail Fisher's Affirmative Action Case Was Really About." *ProPublica*, June 23, 2016. https:// www.propublica.org/article/a-colorblind-constitution-what -abigail-fishers-affirmative-action-case-is-r.

Huffman, James. "The Real Cause of Campus Racism." *The Hoover Institute*, December 15, 2015. http://www.hoover.org/research /real-cause-campus-racism.

Jaschik, Scott. "Tipping Point for Trans Admissions? Smith College Will Now Accept Transgender Applicants Who Identify as

Women. Will Other Women's Colleges Follow?"
Inside Higher Ed, May 4, 2015. https://www.insidehighered.com
/news/2015/05/04/smith-college-will-accept-transgender
-applicants-who-identify-women.

Kaufman, James C. "While Rethinking Admissions Process,
Consider Creativity." *The Conversation*, January 27, 2016. https://
theconversation.com/while-rethinking-admissions
-process-consider-creativity-53675.

Kunthara, Sophia. "South Mountain Community College Pushes
to Correct Course on Graduation and Retention Rates."
Cronkite News, December 30, 2015. https://cronkitenews.azpbs
.org/2015/12/30/south-mountain-community-college-push-
es-to-correct-course-on-graduation-and-retention-rates.

Latham, Patricia H. "Learning Disabilities and The Law: After
High School: An Overview for Students." *Learning Disabilities
Association of America.* https://ldaamerica.org/learning-disabili-
ties-and-the-law-after-high-school-an-overview-for-students-2.

Liversedge, Rosemary. "Patchwork of State Laws Affects
Undocumented Students." *News21*, August 2010. http://asu
.news21.com/2010/08/tuition.

Lueck, Dawn. "The For-Profit College Scam." *Common Dreams*,
May 8, 2015. http://www.commondreams.org/views/2015/05/08
/profit-college-scam.

Marcus, B.K. "Students Don't Need a 'Passion,' They Need
Persistence." *Foundation for Economic Education*, May 4, 2016.
https://fee.org/articles/students-dont-need-a-passion-they
-need-persistence.

McKenna, Joann. "A Dean's Plea: Let Students Discover
Knowledge Without Pressure to Impress." *The Conversation*,
April 29, 2015. https://theconversation.com/a-deans-plea
-let-students-discover-knowledge-without-pressure-to
-impress-40682.

Obama, Barack. "Remarks by the President on Education." *White
House Archives*, October 17, 2016. https://obamawhitehouse
.archives.gov/the-press-office/2016/10/17/remarks
-president-education.

Posselt, Julie Renee. "Turning the Tide: Can Admissions Reforms
Redefine Achievement?" *The Conversation*, January 27, 2016.
https://theconversation.com/turning-the-tide-can-admis-
sions-reforms-redefine-achievement-53686.

Raphel, Alexandra. "Affirmative Action in University Admissions:
Research Roundup." *Journalist's Resource*, December 9, 2015.
https://journalistsresource.org/studies/society/race-society

/affirmative-action-in-university-admissions-research-roundup.

Ramaswamy, Rebecca. R. "Bars to Education: The Use of Criminal History Information in College Admissions." *Columbia Journal of Race and Law*, Volume 5, Issue 2, 2015.

Rauner, Bruce. "Governor Vetoes SB 2043." *Office of the Governor of Illinois*, February 19, 2016. http://www4.illinois.gov/PressReleases/ShowPressRelease.cfm?SubjectID=2&RecNum=13504&SubjectID=2&RecNum=13504.

Staff. *Cannon v. University of Chicago 441 US 677 (1979). Supreme Court of the United States*, May 14, 1979. https://supreme.justia.com/cases/federal/us/441/677.

Staff. "Governor Cuomo Announces $3.2 Million to Promote College Access to Low Income Students." *The New York State Governor's Office*, December 8, 2014. https://www.governor.ny.gov/news/governor-cuomo-announces-32-million-promote-college-access-low-income-students.

Staff. "Governor Vetoes SB 2043." *The Office of the Governor of the State of Illinois*, February 19, 2016. https://www.iml.org/file.cfm?key=7307.

Staff. *Mississippi University for Women v. Hogan 458 US 718 (1982). Supreme Court of the United States*, July 1, 1982. https://supreme.justia.com/cases/federal/us/458/718/case.html.

Sternberg, Robert. "Why 1904 Testing Methods Should Not Be Used for Today's Students." *The Conversation*, November 18, 2015. https://theconversation.com/why-1904-testing-methods-should-not-be-used-for-todays-students-50508.

Thaler, Cynthia. "The Missing 'One-Offs': The Hidden Supply of High-Achieving, Low-Income Students." *Journalist's Resource*, April 17, 2013. https://journalistsresource.org/studies/society/education/missing-one-offs-hidden-supply-high-achieving-low-income-students.

Tucker, Jeffrey. "Is There a Viable Alternative to College?" *Foundation for Economic Education*, July 18, 2013. https://fee.org/articles/is-there-a-viable-alternative-to-college.

Wai, Jonathan and Frank C. Worrell. "A Nation at Risk—How Gifted, Low-Income Kids are Left Behind." *The Conversation*, March 21, 2016. https://theconversation.com/a-nation-at-risk-how-gifted-low-income-kids-are-left-behind-56119.

Wang, Marian. "Admissions Directors at Public Universities Speak Honestly (and Anonymously) About Their Goals." *ProPublica*, September 18, 2013. https://www.propublica.org/article/admissions-directors-at-public-universities-speak-honestly-and-anonymously.

Wang, Marian. "George Washington University Has for Years Claimed to Be 'Need-Blind.' It's Not." *ProPublica*, October 22, 2013. https://www.propublica.org/article/george-washington -university-has-for-years-claimed-to-be-need-blind.-its-not.

Wang, Marian. "The Admission Arms Race: Six Ways Colleges Game Their Numbers." *ProPublica*, April 23, 2013. https://www .propublica.org/article/the-admission-arms-race-six-ways -colleges-can-game-their-numbers.

CHAPTER NOTES

CHAPTER ONE: WHAT THE EXPERTS SAY

"BARS TO EDUCATION: THE USE OF CRIMINAL HISTORY INFORMATION IN COLLEGE ADMISSIONS" BY REBECCA R. RAMAWAMY

*J.D. 2015, Columbia Law School; B.A. 2009, Vassar College. The author would like to thank Professor Susan Sturm for her guidance and the staff of the Columbia Journal of Race and Law for their invaluable editing contributions. The author would also like to thank Aviva Tevah, formerly of the New York Reentry Education Network, for introducing me to this important issue.

1. Center for Community Alternatives, *Passport to the Future: Accessing Higher Education in an Era of Mass* Incarceration, VIMEO (2013), http://vimeo.com/51358967.
2. *See* Roberto Concepción, Jr., *Need Not Apply: The Racial Disparate Impact of Pre-Employment Criminal Background Checks*, 19 GEO. J. ON POVERTY L. & POL'Y 231 (2012).
3. *See* CENTER FOR COMMUNITY ALTERNATIVES, THE USE OF CRIMINAL HISTORY RECORDS IN COLLEGE ADMISSIONS: RECONSIDERED (2010); CENTER FOR COMMUNITY ALTERNATIVES, CLOSING THE DOORS TO HIGHER EDUCATION: ANOTHER COLLATERAL CONSEQUENCE OF A CRIMINAL CONVICTION 4 (2008) ("Examples of state university systems that ask about criminal convictions include North Carolina, Florida and New York").
4. *Id.*
5. *Id.* at 17 ("Convictions for a violent or sex offense are the most likely to trigger an automatic denial of admission").
6. *Id.*
7. *Id.* At 18.
8. *Id.* at 21.
9. *Id.; see also* MICHELLE ALEXANDER, THE NEW JIM CROW: MASS INCARCERATION IN THE AGE OF COLORBLINDNESS (The New Press 2012).

CHAPTER FOUR: WHAT ADVOCATES AND ADVOCACY GROUPS SAY

"HANDLING OBJECTIONS" BY AFRICA S. HANDS, FROM SUCCESSFULLY SERVING THE COLLEGE BOUND

1. US Census Bureau, "American Fact Finder," http://factfinder2.census.gov/faces/nav/jsf/pages/index.html.
2. National Network of Libraries of Medicine, "Libraries and the Affordable Care Act: October 2013," http://guides.nnlm.gov/sea/ACA/
3. Montana State Library, "Affordable Care Act Resources: The Affordable Care Act and Montana Libraries," http://learning.montatastelibrary.org/digitalliterac/Montana-online/afford-able-health-care-act-resources/.
4. Alexandria Walton Radford and Nicole Ifill, "Preparing Student for College: What High Schools Are Doing and How Their Actions Influence Ninth Graders' College Attitudes, Aspirations and Plans: December 2012," National Association for College Admission Counseling, www.nacanet.org/research/research-data/nacac-research/documents/preparing%20students@20for%20college_12-18-12.pdf
5. Ibid.
6. American School Counselor Association, "Student to Counselor Ration 2010-2011," www.schoolcounselor.org/asca/media/asca/home/ratios10-11.pdf.
7. Stephen Betts, "Woodworking and Foreign Language Teachers, Library Staff and Social Worker Among 10 Job Cuts Proposed to Balance Rockland-area School Budget," *Bangor Daily News*, April 17, 2014, http://bangordailynews.com/2014/04/17/news/midcoast/woodworking-and-foreign-language-teachers-library-staff-and-social-worker-among-10-job-cuts-proposed-to-balance-rockland-area-school-budget/.
8. Holly Hines, "ICCSD Teacher Librarians Facing Fallout from Cuts," *Iowa City Press-Citizen*, April 23, 2014, www.press-citizen

.com/story/news/education/k-12/2014/04/24/iccsd-teacher-li-brarians-facing-fallout-cuts/8082003.

9. Teresa Watanabe, "Many L.A. Unified School Libraries, Lacking Staff, Are Forced to Shut," *Los Angeles Times*, February 23, 2014, www.latimes.com/local/la-me-lausd-libraries-20140224-story .html#page=1.

10. Judy Reno, telephone conversation with author, September 2012.

22. Free Library of Philadelphia, "Free Library of College Prep," http://collegeprep.freelibrary.wikispaces.net/About+Us/.

12. Great Lakes Higher Education Corporation, "College Ready Grant," https://community.mygreatlakes.org/web/community /grants/college-ready-grant.html.

GLOSSARY

admissions counselor—These counselors work to recruit applicants and assist in completing paperwork, as well as to establish outreach to high schools or other secondary education programs.

affirmative action—A policy that provides some favor to groups that have been discriminated against, most often on the basis of race.

alma mater—The school or institution from which a student graduates.

alumni—Graduates of a particular institution.

college fairs—Events hosted through schools, colleges, or other institutions where students can meet university and college representatives, learn more about the schools, and ask questions about degree programs or the application process.

college-readiness—The measure of how prepared an applicant is for college, including degree requirements and any particular expectations placed on students.

Common Application—A college application through which students can apply to multiple schools. It is now used by 693 colleges and universities around the world.

express applications—Partially pre-filled applications that have fewer requirements than traditional applications.

financial aid—Grants, scholarships, loans, and other programs offered to assist students in paying for college.

interdisciplinary humanities—Courses like English, Political Science, or Philosophy that are based in the liberal arts and sciences.

laboratory classes—Traditionally, classes that are largely self-guided with little direct assistance.

lecture classes—Courses structured around a professor's lecture or teaching, rather than a self-directed course.

metric—A means by which to measure, such as a test that is used to measure a student's academic performance.

selective schools—Schools that accept students based on academic performance or another set of criteria. Schools that accept all applicants are comprehensive schools.

STEM—An acronym for science, technology, engineering, and math.

test-optional—Schools that do not require standardized test scores, like the SAT, to apply.

Title IX—Passed in the Education Amendments of 1971, this law made it illegal to discriminate based on sex in any education program receiving federal funding.

FOR MORE INFORMATION

BOOKS

Antonoff, Steven R. *College Match: A Blueprint for Choosing the Best School for You.* EDu Consulting Media, 2014.

Belasco, Andrew and Dave Bergman. *The Enlightened College Applicant.* New York: Rowman & Littlefield Publishers, 2016.

Bruni, Frank. *Where You Go Is Not Who You'll Be.* New York: Grand Central Publishing, 2016.

Cipollone, Kristin & Lois Weis & Heather Jenkins. *Class Warfare: Class, Race, and College Admissions in Top-Tier Secondary Schools.* Chicago, IL: University of Chicago Press, 2014.

Espenshade, Thomas J. and Alexandria Walton Radford. *No Longer Separate, Not Yet Equal: Race and Class in Elite College Admission and Campus Life.* Princeton, NJ: Princeton University Press, 2013.

Fisher, Lisa. *Admissions by Design: Stop the Madness and Find the Best College or You.* New York: Elevate, 2016.

Kahlenberg, Richard D. *The Future of Affirmative Action: New Paths to Higher Education Diversity after Fisher v. University of Texas.* New York: The Century Foundation, 2014.

Kaplan, William A. and Barbara A. Lee. *The Law of Higher Education: Student Version.* New York: Jossey-Bass, 2014.

Moore, Meg Mitchell. *The Admissions.* New York: Anchor, 2016.

Ware, Susan. *Title IX: A Brief History with Documents.* Long Grove, IL: Waveland Press, 2014.

WEBSITES

Chronicle of Higher Education
www.chronicle.com
This newspaper is a leading resource for news and analysis about higher education, including admissions and other issues on campus.

Inside Higher Ed
www.insidehighered.com
This website offers news, events, and advice about higher education, including admissions.

NEA: The Higher Education Advocate
www.nea.org
This national education organization publishes work surrounding trends in higher education.

INDEX

ABOUT THE EDITORS

Bridey Heing is a writer and book critic based in Washington, DC. She holds degrees in political science and international affairs from DePaul University and Washington University in Saint Louis. Her areas of focus are comparative politics and Iranian politics. Her master's thesis explores the evolution of populist politics and democracy in Iran since 1900. She has written about Iranian affairs, women's rights, and art and politics for publications like the *Economist*, *Hyperallergic*, and the *Establishment*. She also writes about literature and film. She enjoys traveling, reading, and exploring Washington, DC's many museums.

Greg Baldino holds a bachelor of arts in fiction writing from Columbia College Chicago, where he studied genre literature and twentieth-century social history. He is the author of *Art, Technology, and Language Across the Middle East* and a contributor to the collection *War: The Human Cost*. He lives in Chicago in a converted carriage barn with a vagabond pigeon.